The Frankenste... Show

Book by John Crocker and Tim Hampton

Music by Ken Bolam

Lyrics by Les Scott

Samuel French – London
New York – Sydney – Toronto – Hollywood

CHARACTERS

A Corpse
Igor, a manservant
Mrs Beatrice Body, the housekeeper
John B. Good, a solicitor
Frank Enstein
Boris
Willie Burke ⎫ undertakers
Willie Hare ⎭
Mrs Leucretia Burkenhare, their wife
Dr Ruby Watson
Sherlock Holmes, Junior
Firing Squad Officer
American Tourists
Police Inspector
Myriad Monsters

MUSICAL NUMBERS

ACT I

1	**Overture**	Orchestra
2	**Spooky Incidental**	Orchestra
3a–e	**Discords—Revealing of Monsters**	Orchestra
4	**Humanoid Boogie**	Corpse and Monsters
5	**Enstein's the Name**	Frank
6	**Spooky Incidental**	Orchestra
7	**Sting—Thinks!**	Orchestra
8	**Every Home Should Have a Happy Healthy Monster**	Frank, Igor, Mrs Body and Boris
9	**Every Home Should Have a Happy Healthy Monster** (Reprise)	Frank, Igor, Mrs Body, Burke, Hare and Mrs Burkenhare
10a	**Shimmer**	Orchestra
10b	**Can This Be Love?**	John and Ruby
11	**Soft Funereal Incidental**	Orchestra
12	**I'm Only Monstrous**	Boris
13a	**New Technology—Dramatic chord**	Orchestra
13b	**Activation—tremolo,** continuing under dialogue	Orchestra
13c	**Total Built-in Control**	Frank and Monsters
14	**There Must Be a Way**	Company

ACT II

15	**Business Is Big**	Mrs Burkenhare, Mrs Body, Igor and Monsters
16	**Business Was Small**	Igor and Mrs Body
17	**Elementary**	Sherlock
18a	**Spooky Incidental**	Orchestra
18b	**Gaily, Daily, Dealing Out Death**	Burke and Hare
19	**Put Your Head Upon the Block**	Tourists, Burke, Hare, Igor and Mrs Body
20	**Chase Incidental**	Orchestra
21	**Shall I Ever See My Love Again?**	John and Ruby
22	**This Is My Way to Make a Man**	Mrs Burkenhare
23	**Finale Medley**	Company

PRODUCTION NOTES

The style of playing required for this show is broad but sincere. Each character should entirely believe in him or herself, but be played with a good deal of relish so that it is just that much larger than life and achieves a kind of cartoon quality. Any tendency to over-indulgence must be avoided, though, since it will only slacken the pace and that should never be less than brisk.

Corpse Only a small part but one needing considerable authority. The character displays something of the dedication of the fanatic.

Igor A confirmed traditionalist who, though obviously old and querulous, can also be surprisingly lively.

Mrs Body A comfortable old soul, but with a few sharp edges; she is also slightly inclined towards hypochondria. She provides a natural foil for **Igor**'s quainter qualities.

John B. Good An innocent who tries hard and means well. If that sounds too damning he should also have a naïve kind of charm which appeals not only to **Ruby**, but also the audience.

Frank Enstein An American dynamo. His outlook is not so much evil as blinkered—he has a single-minded devotion to a single idea. He should also have great sex appeal, of which he is entirely unaware.

Boris He should look as alike as possible to the Boris Karloff model and just as frightening. His nature, though, is benign for, whatever qualities were inherent in his component parts, malice was not one of them. However, like a child, he can be subject to tantrums, which are fiery but short-lived.

Burke and **Hare** A couple of endearing idiots who happen to be Irish—but only because the original Burke and Hare were. Essentially a twosome and essentially henchmen. **Burke** is the cleverer of the pair—or at least thinks he is. **Hare** does not think about it—or anything else much.

Mrs Burkenhare A voluptuous seductress with two interests in her life, money and sex—in that order. Clever and sophisticated, she is the business brains behind the organization and always has an eye to the main chance.

Dr Ruby Watson Very attractive, but with a briskness often associated with doctors. This gives her a practical, no-nonsense approach to life—until she meets **John**. Her reaction to him is entirely irrational; but then falling in love is.

Sherlock Holmes Junior He has tried to acquire all his famous forebear's attributes in an obsessive attempt to outdo him. He is thwarted in this ambition by only one thing—he's a fool. So, convinced of his genius, he invariably grasps the wrong end of every stick that life proffers.

Monsters   There can be as many as are available and desirable for any given production. Sex and colour are immaterial, the only essential is that they should always look like monsters with the exception of the **Police**—and that can be achieved by make-up and a uniformity of stilted and awkward movement.

Staging

The directions in the script assume a tab surround, with a curtained alcove upstage (which ideally should be raised), and a set of traverse tabs to help ensure swift and unobtrusive scene changes. Into this basic setting door-ways, furniture and dressing can be fitted as required. The various signs flown in will only need very shallow flying space. Their use not only conveys information—such as a change of locale—but can also contribute to the cartoon quality mentioned earlier.

The foregoing is only intended as a suggestion of one, fairly simple, way to present the show, but imaginative directors can, of course, develop any other ideas that best suit their available resources.

Certain items perhaps need special mention:

Trick Coffin   A frame constructed in conventional coffin shape with hardboard panels attached, apart from the upstage panel to allow the **Corpse** to slip out. The space is covered on the inside of the coffin with black material tacked to the top of the frame. The coffin can be doubled for use in Act I, Scene 3.

Prop Corpse   As nearly as possible a life-size facsimile of the actor. It is pre-set under him.

Machine   A simple box shape which can be made of flats cleeted or pin-hinged together. Suitable dials, switches, levers and lights (practical) are fitted on to it. It needs an opening at either end and to be set so that characters can enter it unseen from offstage. The onstage opening could be covered with a metal strip curtain.

Four-legged, No-headed, No-armed Monster   Two false legs stick up in the air from a covered frame which represents half an upside-down torso. It fits over the head and on to the shoulders of the actor concerned, whose arms go into the legs to operate them. A gauze panel must be inserted at eye level.

Electric Chair   A solid, square-shaped wooden chair, fitted with wrist and ankle straps, wire coils, tube lights and a lever.

Execution Axe   The head is shaped out of thick foam rubber.

Guillotine   A frame with grooved sides in which a wedge-shaped blade can ride up and down. The blade can be made of painted hardboard or aluminium sheet attached to a bar, in the centre of which is a rope running over a pulley at the top of the frame. The bottom of the blade's descent is hidden by the screen.

Shots   It may well be difficult to get licences for sufficient blank rifles and pistols, so we have listed each salvo in the Effects Plot to give the noise required.

ACT I

Music 1: Overture

SCENE 1

Enstein Hall

On a darkened stage the traverse tabs are closed. In front of them is a table on which a trick coffin is set (see Production Notes)

Music 2: Spooky Incidental

The music is rather spooky and is accompanied by howling wind and general storm effects. A Spot comes up on the coffin. Slowly the lid rises—so does an ancient Corpse

Corpse Good-evening. I'm dead. How are you? I haven't always been dead, of course. No, no! And if I wasn't dead now I could bring myself to life again. Because I made a great discovery—how to create life! I made a man, perfect in every detail——

Music 3a: Dramatic Discord

A Spot comes up R on a typical Frankenstein Monster, with bolts and stitching

Well almost. And where I've led, others will follow. Where I made one, they'll make two——

Music 3b: Discord

A Spot comes up on two Monsters L

Or three——

Music 3c: Discord

A Spot comes up on a third Monster L

Or more!

Music 3d: Discord

A Spot comes up on a fourth Monster L

More I said, not four! Lots more!

Music 3e: Discord

Lights up on as many Monsters as can be mustered

Thank you. And all walking, talking, just like you!

Music 4: Humanoid Boogie

The Monsters spring into life when the music starts

(*Singing*)	Eat, drink, breathe, think,
	Run, hop, lean, blink.
	The Humanoid Boogie's
	Coming home to roost.
	Jump, stride, squirm, walk,
	Shout, scream, nod, talk,
	It's really something else,
	It's gonna be a hoot.
Monsters	Going,
	We want to dance and sing.
	Dancing,
	We're not an awful thing.
	We've come alive and we're feeling new,
	We're walking, talking, just like you, just like you.
All	Walking, talking, walking, talking,
	Just like you, just like you.
	Walking, talking, walking, talking,
	Just like you, just like you.
	Humanoid, Humanoid Boogie, Humanoid, Humanoid
	Boogie,
	Humanoid, Humanoid Boogie, Humanoid.
	Humanoid, Humanoid Boogie, Humanoid, Humanoid
	Boogie,
	Humanoid, Humanoid Boogie, Humanoid.

Kick, prance, look, glance,
Skip, trot, sigh, dance,
Frankenstein Monsters
Celebrate in style.
Knock, chat, bend, tap,
Sit, lie, wish, rap,
It's really something else
Now we've come alive.

Going,
We want to dance and sing,
Dancing,
We're not an awful thing.

We've come alive and we're feeling new,
We're walking, talking, just like you, just like you.
Walking, talking, walking, talking,
Just like you, just like you.
Walking, talking, walking, talking,
Just like you, just like you.
Humanoid, Humanoid Boogie, Humanoid, Humanoid
    Boogie,
Humanoid, Humanoid Boogie, Humanoid.
Humanoid, Humanoid Boogie, Humanoid, Humanoid
    Boogie,
Humanoid, Humanoid Bookie, Humanoid.
Humanoid, Humanoid Boogie, Humanoid, Humanoid
    Boogie,
Humanoid, Humanoid Boogie, Humanoid.

The Monsters disappear as the Lights fade and the music dies away

The single spot is left on the coffin and the Corpse climbs back into it

Corpse Ah, not yet, not yet. All just a dead man's dream. Or is it . . .?

He lowers the lid and the Spot fades to Black-out. The Corpse gets out of the back of the coffin and exits unseen as the traverse tabs open

Lightning flash and a loud crack of thunder

The Lights come up as Igor, an ancient retainer, totters on from L with a candle

The décor revealed should suggest a heavy Victorian Gothic interior. There is a door L, a front door R and a curtained alcove UC. More lightning and thunder

Igor Ah, what a lovely night!

Mrs Beatrice Body enters L, working hard at trying to feel a pain in her back

Mrs Body Lovely? It's not lovely for my twinges. It brings them on. You wouldn't think it was lovely if you had my twinges.
Igor Well, I haven't, so I do. Lovely.

More lightning and thunder. He looks hopefuly at the coffin

Enough to wake the dead.
Mrs Body Twaddle. Just wishful thinking, Igor.
Igor Maybe, but I remember another night like this. Another night when the old master——
Mrs Body He's not the old master now, he's the dead master. So we must prepare for the new one. He may be here any minute. You heard what the lawyer told us just now in the library.
Igor Lawyer? That young—young——
Mrs Body Exactly. Young Mr Good, of Good, Better and Best.
Igor And why can't we have old Mr Good, like we always used to?
Mrs Body Because he's dead, too.

Igor I don't care, he should have been here. Shows more respect. But that young whipper-snapper just talked a lot of rubbish. All that stuff about the new Mr Enstein.
Mrs Body What, about him being old Mr E.'s great-great-nephew and only surviving relative?
Igor No, no, the other bit. About him being born in America. I mean, fancy letting himself be born in America. And then all that rigmarole about being a commuter expert in rheumatics.
Mrs Body Not commuter—computer. And it wasn't rheumatics, it was robotics.
Igor Same thing. Lot of new-fangled nonsense. Robotics, huh! What are robotics, anyway?
Mrs Body Something to do with making robots, of course. You know, sort of man-made men.
Igor Man-made men! You mean, like ...? (*He nods his head vigorously upstage*)
Mrs Body No robots are machines, not at all like ... (*She nods her head upstage equally vigorously*)
Igor Shall we tell the new master about ...? (*He nods upstage even more vigorously*)
Mrs Body No! Not yet, anyway.
Igor Well, of course not yet. He's not here yet.

There is a loud knocking at the front door R

Both He is!
Mrs Body The new master!
Igor At the door!
Both Knocking!

John B. Good enters L, carrying a briefcase

John I say ...
Igor (*very frigidly*) Yes, Mr Good?
John Isn't there someone at the door?
Igor Possibly.

The knocking increases. Igor opens the door to reveal Frank Enstein

Yes.

He shuts the door, but Frank thrusts it open, knocking Igor aside, and enters

Frank Hi. Enstein's the name. Frank Enstein.

Lightning, thunder

Music 5: Enstein's the Name

(*Singing*) I'm a scientist it's true,
I study ions, molecules,
I have means to study genes
And I follow Newton's rules.

I know I'm on to something big!
I have researched protozoa,
Roamin' through the haemoglobin,
For a form of life that's lower.

I know of chromium and cadmium,
Samarium and helium,
Polonium, potassium,
Tellurium and caesium —
It's really elementary.
Frank Enstein's the name
And I'm from the USA,
From research in DNA.

I have scoured many books,
I have studied many topics,
No illusions re conclusions,
There's a future in robotics.
I know I'm on to something big!
I have researched protozoa,
Roamin' through the haemoglobin,
For a form of life that's lower, lower, lower, lower, lower.

I know of chromium and cadmium ... *etc.*

I'm a scientist it's true,
Let me know of any queries,
Conclusions or illusions
Concerning Enstein's theories.
I know I'm on to something big!
I have researched protozoa,
Roamin' through the haemoglobin,
For a form of life that's lower, lower, lower, lower, lower.

I know of chromium and cadmium ... *etc.*

OK. You caught the name? Enstein. Frank Enstein.

Lightning, thunder

Is the weather always this bad round here?
Igor Of course! It would be!
Frank What, the weather?
Igor No, your first name, sir. Frank. All the male Ensteins have been called Frank, ever since ...
John Really? Ever since when?
Igor Ah, lost in the mists of time.
Mrs Body So are you, you old fool. Rambling on when we should be welcoming Mr Enstein.
John Quite right, Mrs Body. I'm John B. Good, Mr Enstein.
Frank Great to know you, John. (*He pumps John's hand vigorously*)
John Ooh! Aah! Yes, thank you. (*He retrieves his hand and finds it rather limp*) Great-er-pleasure. I'm your solicitor.

Frank Solici—? Oh, my attorney—sure. And who's this little guy?

John That little guy is—I mean, that is Igor. And this is Mrs Body.

Mrs Body Mrs Beatrice Body, sir. (*She bobs a curtsy*) Your housekeeper.

Frank Housekeeper? Gee, that's tough, Beattie baby.

Mrs Body (*startled, but pleased*) Beattie baby!

Frank 'Cos you're not gonna have a house to keep. I'm selling the place.

Mrs Body What!

Igor Selling Enstein Hall!

John But why? What for?

Frank Money. I aim to start my own business making computerized robots. And that takes bread—a lot of bread.

John But you've got—er—bread. All of old Mr Enstein's—bread. Oodles of it.

Frank That's great because I'm no business man, I'm a scientist, but a good one—what I don't know about computerized robot systems isn't worth knowing. In time I'll conquer the world—and nothing and nobody's gonna stop me. But I have to get started and to do that I can't have too much bread. So the house—it goes. Fix it for me, John.

John Well, if you really . . . of course, but——

Frank And soon. Like tomorrow, maybe.

John T-tomorrow?

Frank (*leading him to the front door*) Yeah, now before you go——

John Go?

Frank Sure, to get started. There's just one small detail——how much have I been left? You said there was——?

John Oodles.

Frank Great, but what's the going rate for an oodle?

John Ah, the precise amount. Er—wouldn't you rather I told you confidentially?

Frank OK. Confidentially. Whisper.

John (*shrugging then getting out some papers*) It's a little complicated. You see, there's . . . (*He whispers*)

Frank gives increasingly pleased reactions during John's speech, which should only be a background to Mrs Body's and Igor's dialogue

And then there's . . . (*he whispers*). But not forgetting . . . (*he whispers*). Oh, and I almost did forget—where is it now? Ah, yes. (*He whispers*) Which, together with . . . (*he whispers*). So, all in all, and allowing for death duties, of course, it'll be something in the region of . . . (*he whispers*).

Mrs Body Igor, what are we to do? What's to become of us?

Igor Never mind us. What about . . .? (*He nods upstage*)

Mrs Body Oh yes, what about . . .? (*She nods upstage*)

Igor All that work . . . all that knowledge, it mustn't be wasted. Ah, maybe . . . he said he's a scientist—it's worth a try—we'll show him the notebook!

Mrs Body The notebook! Yes! Where is it? There?

She nods upstage as Frank turns, emitting a low whistle of pleasure as he learns the final sum

Igor No, there. (*He nods towards the coffin*)
Frank You folks seem kinda twitchy.
Igor Ah—we were just discussing—er—where to put your chair, sir. For the vigil.
Frank The vigil?
John Golly, yes. The vigil. That's a condition of your inheritance—you have to keep vigil by the corpse. If you don't——
Frank No bread?
John Not a crumb.

A deep-toned bell begins to chime the hour

Midnight! I must be going. Good-night.

He exits swiftly through the front door

Igor
Mrs Body } (*together*) The vigil!

As the clock starts to strike 12 slowly, Igor places a chair by the DL *corner of the coffin and Mrs Body leads a rather doubtful Frank to it. As the last stroke sounds Igor opens the coffin lid. It creaks*

Frank Jeepers! (*Starting to rise*) I don't——
Mrs Body (*pushing him down*) We've something to show you, sir.
Frank (*gulping*) Him?
Igor No. This. (*He takes out an ancient book and hands it to Frank*) A bit of family history.
Mrs Body Right up your street as a scientist.
Igor Yes, sort of early commuter rheumatics.
Frank What?
Mrs Body It's all in the book, sir.
Frank This is a helluva way to spend a night.

Lightning and thunder crash

Music 6: Spooky Incidental

Muted thunder rumblings continue under the music

And what a night.

Igor Yes, what a night. Just like the night when——
Mrs Body Ssh. It's in the book.
Igor But will it save us?
Mrs Body Maybe.
Igor Will it save Boris?
Mrs Body It might.
Igor And if it does——?
Mrs Body If it does——!

Lightning and thunder crash. Frank jumps up, very excited

Frank This is incredible!
Mrs Body |
Igor | (*together*) Yes!
Frank Fantastic!!
Mrs Body |
Igor | (*together*) Yes!!
Frank Impossible!!!
Mrs Body |
Igor | (*together*) No!!!

The music ends with a dramatic chord as they pull open the alcove curtains to reveal an old-fashioned laboratory, bristling with ancient and cumbersome electrical equipment. On a table in the centre lies the huge form of Boris, (very much à la Karloff), with electrodes attached to his knees, his feet, his elbows and one temple

Frank Holy Moses!
Igor No, Boris.
Frank You mean—the original ...?
Mrs Body The one and only!
Frank And he's all plugged in—just throw a couple of switches and—bingo! Hold it. Where's the electric supply lead?
Igor Electrics! We don't have any truck with electrics here.
Mrs Body No, we can give you another candle, though.
Frank A candle! How can I reanimate him with a candle? Don't answer that. Landsakes, all this and no electricity. Then how in Hades——?

Lightning flash and thunder

Of course! The original galvanizing method! (*Hastily he turns pages in the book*) Got it! Igor, Beattie! We must be ready for the next flash. Check the electrodes. Metatarsal?
Igor Meta-what, sir?
Frank Tarsal.
Igor (*starting to look*) I don't think he's——
Frank His feet!
Igor Oh! Yes.
Frank Patella—knees?
Mrs Body |
Igor | (*together*) Yes.
Frank Arms?
Mrs Body |
Igor | (*together*) Yes.
Frank Head?
Mrs Body | (*together*) Yes.
Igor | Ye——no!
Igor It's come away. Er—oh well. (*He sticks the loose electrode into Boris's ear*) Right.
Frank OK. Now, lightning conductor. (*He engages a lever*) DC transformer. (*He engages a second lever*) And induction galvanizer when the

lightning strikes. (*He puts his hand on a third lever. A slight pause. He looks heavenwards*) Aw, come on, come on!

Mrs Body I think the storm's passing over.

Tremendous lightning flash and thunder clap

Frank All systems go!

He pushes home the third lever. Lights flicker, cacophony of electronic noises, fizzles and some smoke. Boris quivers violently all over until there is a loud explosion. All move hastily away, then come back cautiously and stare at Boris, who now seems quite inert. Frank throws down the book

Hogwash! I should have known that it——

Boris suddenly sits up with an awesome groan

It works!

Boris I'm hungry.

Frank Hungry? You want more electricity? Heck, you've just had twenty thousand volts.

Boris Somebody connected me up wrong. How'd you like it if someone stuffed food down your earhole?

Mrs Body looks accusingly at Igor

Igor You must be more careful, Beatrice. Still, no harm done. Good, isn't he?

Frank We-ll—he's certainly an amazing concept.

Boris I'm not a concept. I'm a monster.

Frank No comment. Can he walk?

Boris Course I can walk. (*He swings off the table and walks with very stiff legs and his arms held out in front of him*) See?

Frank Yeah. It's not exactly natural, though.

Boris Ah, this is my special walk. People expect it of me. But I can walk ordinary too. Look. (*He draws himself up, puts his arms down, but otherwise walks exactly as before*) Ordinary, isn't it?

Frank Oh, sure. Say, those bolts in his neck——

Igor Don't worry, they're very firm. I fixed 'em myself.

Frank And all that stitching.

Mrs Body (*proudly*) Yes, I learnt to sew on Boris.

Frank And the top of his head. It's too flat.

Boris It's not flat. It's just flattering.

He ho-hos hollowly and Igor and Mrs Body crease up

Igor That's his joke.

Frank Boris, there's only one thing wrong with you. You're dumb.

Boris Not when I'm talking I'm not.

Frank This is ridiculous. Here we have a dazzling leap forward in scientific thinking, a staggering short-cut in computerized robotics, a simple but brilliant idea—to use the most efficient material available for component parts—the human anatomy itself! And this stupendous, this awesome, this mind-boggling solution is used to create what? An idiot!

Boris (*amiably*) Who's an idiot?

Frank You are.

Boris stiffens. Mrs Body and Igor exchange a look and start to back away

What waste! What criminal stupidity! What—— (*He notices Igor and Mrs Body*) Where are you going?

Igor You shouldn't have said that, sir. Boris doesn't——

Boris starts to move heavily towards Frank

Run!

Frank turns and sees Boris, then starts to back round the coffin, getting faster and faster, while Igor runs to the front door and Mrs Body to the library door to hide behind them and then to peer round them fearfully

Frank Hey now, take it easy, Boris.

Boris Idiot! Me? I'm clever.

Frank Sure—sure——

Boris I'll show you how clever I am. I'll undo you. Bit by bit.

Frank Now, Boris, get back. Stay! Down, boy! Heel—no! Si*t*!

Boris suddenly collapses on his table

Well, whadday'know?

Igor and Mrs Body re-emerge

You needn't have worried. I found the right technique, he responded.

Igor Yes. He also ran out of juice.

Frank Oh. How do you control him then?

Mrs Body You don't. Not if he really gets going.

Frank But there's gotta be control. It only needs a simple micro circuit. With that you could do anything with him. It's so straightforward, so easy.

Music 7: Sting—Thinks!

Yeah, it's easy, but it's revolutionary. Why should it stop at him? We know the basic method, apply that to a modern production line and we could turn them out by the hundred—the thousand! Every home could have one! Not only could—should!

Music 8: Every Home Should Have a Happy, Healthy Monster

(*Singing*)   Every home should have a happy, healthy monster,
                 Every home should have a happy, healthy zomb'.
                 So buy if you dare,
                 For you won't care
                 Who's that man over there.

They'll do a job in a jiffy,
They'll do it on the spot.
Monsters do what they're told,
They throw out what is old.

They can do the chores,
They can wash the floors.

Igor   They can pay your bills,
              They can check your tills.

Mrs Body They can make you laugh,
              They can fill your bath.

Boris   They can bake a cake,
              They can use a rake.

Frank   They can sew your jeans,
              They can warm up beans.

Igor   They can make the toast,
              They can cook a roast.

Mrs Body They can feed the cat,
              They can brush your hat.

Boris   They can wash your hair,
              They can sweep the stair.

All   That's why—
              Every home should have ... etc.

Frank   They'll do a job in a jiffy,
              They'll do it on the spot.
              Monsters do what they're told,
              They throw out what is old.

They can fix a plug,
They can fill a jug.

Igor   They can starch a shirt,
              They can sweep the dirt.

Mrs Body They can darn a sock,
              They can seam a frock.

Boris   They can make a bed,
              They can comb your head.

Frank   They can do the chores,
              They can wash the floors.

Igor   They can pay your bills,
              They can check your tills.

Mrs Body They can make you laugh,
              They can fill your bath.

Boris   They can bake a cake,
              They can use a rake.

All   Every home should have ... etc.

Every home should have a happy, healthy,
Every home should have a happy, healthy,
Every home should have a happy, healthy monster.

At the end of the number Boris subsides on to the table and Igor and Mrs Body close the alcove curtains

Frank That's it! We got it made! We got—hell! We got a problem. Where we gonna get the raw material?

There are three very deliberate knocks at the front door. Igor opens it to disclose Burke and Hare, dressed in sober black

Hare (*very Irish*) Good-evening, we are——
Burke Messrs Burke——
Hare And Hare——
Burke }
Hare } (*together*) Undertakers. At your service.
Frank Undertakers? Undertakers! WOWEE!

Burke and Hare are surprised, Igor and Mrs Body severely disapproving, until Frank draws them aside and whispers first to Igor then to Mrs Body

Igor Whoopee!
Mrs Body Yipee!
Burke (*to Hare*) It must be a wake.
Burke }
Hare } (*together, leaping into the room and starting to jig*) Yahoo!

       With a toot on the flute
       And a twiddle on the fiddle-o——
Burke (*noticing the others' stony faces and petering out*)
       Hopping in the middle . . . like a herring . . .

       This is a sad and solemn moment.
Hare Up, down, hands around, crossing——

Burke nudges him fiercely

       Very sad, to be sure. But then, in the midst of death we are in life. (*To Burke*) Aren't we?

Burke is confused too

Frank Buster, you hit the button right on the nose. So I'll sock it to you straight. All those corpses. We know what you do with them.
Burke |
Hare | (*together, worried*) You do?
Frank We do and it's wrong——
Igor It's wicked——
Mrs Body It's criminal.
Burke }
Hare } (*to each other*) They do!
Frank I mean—all those *bones*. Course I don't want to make a *meal* out of this——
Burke (*to Hare*) Bones!
Hare (*to Burke*) Meal!

Burke
Hare } (*together*) The bonemeal deal!

Igor And all that flesh—but what do you get out of it? Not a sausage.

Burke
Hare } (*to each other*) The sausage factory!

Mrs Body You don't even get the hair to pay.

Burke
Hare } (*to each other*) Toupets! The wig emporium!

Burke (*to Hare*) They know everything!

Hare (*to Burke*) We're done for!

Burke (*to Frank*) All right. How much?

Frank How much what?

Burke How much to keep quiet about the bonemeal, the sausages and the wigs?

Frank What bonemeal, what—? Oh! *That* bonemeal!

Igor *Those* sausages!

Mrs Body *Those* wigs!

Hare You hit the nose right on the belly button.

Frank I'll tell you. It won't cost you a dime.

Burke
Hare } (*together*) It won't?

Frank No, you just shut down your whole operation——

Burke
Hare } (*together*) What!!??

Frank And supply to me—exclusively. Starting with Great-Uncle. I'm not having him end up as bonemeal——

Igor Or sausages——

Mrs Body Or a wig.

Frank He's gonna be the foundation of something new, something big. But we gotta play it cool. Beattie baby, where's the refrigera—hell, no electricity. Well, somewhere good and cold.

Mrs Body There's only the larder, sir.

Frank OK, the larder. Lift him out, boys.

Burke and Hare lift a prop corpse from the coffin

Igor Oh sir, the old master—in the larder ...

Frank Sure, he's got the place of honour. The beginning of our stock-pile. He's getting right in on the ground floor.

Igor It's down in the basement.

Frank Don't quibble, Igor. Shift your ass and get him down there.

Igor and Mrs Body huffily lead the way off L

Boys—what do I call you?

Burke
Hare } (*together*) Willie.

Frank Both of you?

Burke
Hare } (*together*) Both of us.

Frank Fine. Well, Willies, this is a whole new ball game for you. I'll just explain the rules.

Frank, Burke and Hare exit L

A slight pause, then a tentative tap at the front door. Another pause and the tap is repeated more firmly. After another moment John puts his head round the door

John I say . . . I just remembered I've forgotten——Oh. Nobody here? (*He enters fully*) No, nobody. Not a living soul. (*He glances in the empty coffin as he passes*) Or a dead one. (*He swivels round and does an enormous take on the coffin*) Gosh! Where? What? Who? Grave robbers! No. He's not dead then? He . . . I must find somebody—anybody!

He rushes to the door L, *just as it is thrust open to knock him out of sight as Frank, Burke, Hare, Igor and Mrs Body stream on*

Frank OK, you got the picture. Now I'll show you the clincher—Boris. I'll get him going while you shift that.

Burke (*shutting the lid*) Aw, it's a lovely coffin, Willie.

Hare It is so, Willie. (*To Frank*) Did you want it buried or cremated?

Frank Both and hang the expense.

He disappears swiftly behind the alcove curtains. Burke and Hare lift the coffin with ease and are moving briskly R *as John emerges with a groan, holding his nose and obviously a little dazed*

Igor Mr Good!

Burke and Hare stop momentarily and look back, then simulate suitable weight in the coffin and continue off R *more decorously*

John Hey, what are those chaps doing?

Igor Just taking old Mr Enstein to his final larder—er, resting place.

John But old Mr Enstein's not there.

Mrs Body No, sir, he's gone now.

John I know he's gone, but where?

Igor Ah, who can say? Either up——

Mrs Body Or down. (*Looking off* L) I just hope it's not too hot for him down there.

John Who are those chaps?

Igor The undertakers, sir.

John I can see that, but I'm sure I've seen them before somewhere and not—well, not undertaking.

Frank appears through the curtains. Igor and Mrs Body try unobtrusively to draw his attention to John

Frank Whaddayaknow? Great-uncle built in a kinda electrostatic charger. I just plugged in—(*he registers John*)—my rechargable razor. Yeah . . . would you two look after my *rechargable razor*?

Igor and Mrs Body nod knowingly and disappear into the alcove

Something you wanted, Mr Good?

John Yes, the deeds. I forgot them. I need them to sell the house.
Frank Sell the house? No way. I'm not selling. I'm expanding.
John But you said——
Frank Sure, but that was before I knew what this place had going for it. Like—er—well, the larder.
John The larder?
Frank Yeah, great larder. You should see—no, maybe you shouldn't.

Burke and Hare enter through the front door

Anyway, I gotta discuss some things with Mr Burke and Mr Hare so, nice talking to you, but 'bye now.
John Eh? Oh, of course—er—goodbye. Burke and Hare, eh? Excuse me, have you always been undertakers?
Burke We-ll—we've a long family connection with that line of business.
John Ah. Right. Thanks.

John exits through the front door

Frank What's his interest in you guys? He a client of yours?
Hare No. We'd remember if we'd buried him.
Burke Yes, you see we don't handle the live clients, only the dead ones. It's Mrs Burkenhare who fixes all the business details.
Frank Who's Mrs Burkenhare?

Off R there is the sound of a car approaching very fast, followed by a scream of brakes and the slam of a car door

Burke ⎫
Hare ⎬ (*together*) That's Mrs Burkenhare.

Frank But who *is* Mrs Burkenhare?

Mrs Burkenhare enters R

Mrs Burkenhare I am.
Burke ⎫
Hare ⎬ (*together*) Meet the wife.

Burke (*pointing to himself*) Monday to Wednesday.
Hare (*pointing to himself*) Thursday to Saturday.
Mrs Burkenhare I like to keep my Sundays free.
Frank Sounds a novel arrangement.
Mrs Burkenhare No, it's more of a tax arrangement.
Burke Two dodges for the price of one. Now, my little darling——
Hare It's Thursday. She's my little darling.
Burke All right, you tell her.
Hare Tell her what?
Burke What I was going to tell her.
Hare How do I know what you were going to tell her?
Frank I think what your husbands want to say is that I've got a proposition for you.
Mrs Burkenhare I'm sure I'd be very interested in any proposition you care to make.

Frank Swell. Now your husbands have agreed to closing down your—er—your little sidelines and supplying to me exclusively.

Mrs Burkenhare Boys, what have you got us into?

Hare Well, it's a whole new game of balls.

Mrs Burkenhare Really?

Frank Yeah, I could see you people had never thought of recycling.

Burke Cycling? I don't think the customers would like that—not with the hearse.

Mrs Burkenhare Pay no attention to them, I never do. What sort of recycling?

Frank Maybe I'd better show you a sample of my end product.

Mrs Burkenhare Your end product?

Frank Yeah. Boris.

There is a roar from Boris in the alcove

Burke ⎱ (*together*) Glory be! What's that?
Hare ⎰

Igor ⎱ (*together, in the alcove*) Boris!
Mrs Body ⎰

Boris thrusts open the curtains and enters with Igor and Mrs Body trying to pull him back. Burke and Hare retreat

Mrs Burkenhare What a monster!

Boris I'm still hungry.

Burke Save us! What's he eat?

Hare I think he's got his eye on us.

Mrs Body Boris, behave. We've got company.

Boris They're not company for me. I'm lonely. I want another me. The other sort of me. (*He indicates the outline of a bosom*) I've always wanted one of them.

Frank Don't worry, Boris. We're gonna make so many sorts of you you'll be spoilt for choice. Like I said——

Music 9: Every Home Should Have a Happy, Healthy Monster (Reprise)

The traverse tabs close as the reprise starts. During the song, the stage is re-set (see Furniture and Property List) and John enters to sit at the desk

(*Singing*)	Every home should have a happy, healthy monster,
	Every home should have a happy, healthy zomb'.
	So buy if you dare,
	For you won't care
	Who's that man over there.
All	They'll do a job in a jiffy,
	They'll do it on the spot.
	Monsters do what they're told,
	They throw out what is old.
Frank	They can do the chores,
	They can wash the floors.

Igor	They can pay your bills,
	They can check your tills.
Mrs Body	They can make you laugh,
	They can fill your bath.
Boris	They can bake a cake,
	They can use a rake.
Hare	They can dig a hole,
	They can rock and roll.
Burke	They can dig a grave,
	They can really rave.
Mrs Burkenhare	They can dig a ditch,
	They can make us rich.
All	They can show us how,
	They can be a wow!

Every home should have ... *etc.*

Every home should have a happy, healthy,
Every home should have a happy, healthy,
Every home should have a happy, healthy monster.

All exit

The tabs open partially to reveal a notice hanging down—"Good, Better &
Best, Solicitors", over a desk at which John is seated looking very perplexed

John Burke and Hare? Hare and Burke? Hurke and Bare? No! Come along
now, put the old thinking cap on. You know you've seen them before,
only where? Not at a funeral—in court maybe? Yes, in court! Something
to do with the Office of Fair Trading and all that ... Overcharging on
funerals? Unlikely. Second-hand hearse dealers? No. Think, think!

The Light fades on John and the tabs close. There is the sound of muffled
thumpings and bangings off L. *The Lights come up* DS

Mrs Body (*off* L, *rather breathless*) Igor, stop! We're too old to be doing this.
Igor (*off* L, *also breathless*) Nonsense, it's just awkward on the stairs.

They enter, carrying the prop corpse

You see, it's easy on the level.
Mrs Body Not with my twinges, it isn't. And where are we going to put
him?
Igor Anywhere, but I'm not leaving the old master in the larder. The idea!
Using him to make Borises.

They exit R. *Frank hurries on* L, *followed by Boris*

Boris Here, have you made that other sort for me yet?
Frank Not yet, Boris. Very busy just now. But I will later. Yeah, later.

They exit R

The Lights fade DS *and a light comes up on John and the tabs partially open*

John Cut-price crypts? No. Worm-eaten coffins? No, no. Obviously

nothing to do with undertakers—*under*takers? Under—underweight ...
underweight sausages! That's it! Not enough in their sausages. Just like
their coffins. Good Lord! There couldn't be a connection, could there?
No, no—impossible. But then again—possible. Got to protect my client's
interests. I need help. A detective agency. (*He picks up a copy of Yellow
Pages and opens it*) Ah, what a bit of luck. (*Reading*) "Discreet inquiries
... satisfaction guaranteed ... proved and traditional methods ...
Sherlock Holmes—Junior?"

Black-out

SCENE 2

221z Baker Street

*There are doors L and R. RC is a desk. A portrait of a solid Victorian-looking
gentleman hangs upstage. We hear the sound of a violin being played off R,
excruciatingly badly*

*There is a tap at the door L, then Dr Ruby Watson, an attractive-looking
young woman, looks round it. She carries a file of papers*

Ruby Mr Holmes? Mr Holmes! Are you there, Mr Holmes?

*The violin stops and an aged gentleman wearing a deerstalker cap and an
Inverness cape over his pyjamas and puffing furiously at a large calabash
pipe, propels himself on from R in a wheelchair*

Sherlock Certainly. Sherlock Holmes, Junior, at your service.
Ruby Thank you. I am——
Sherlock No need to tell me, I know. You are a solicitor and you've just
come from Lincoln's Inn Fields on a number twenty-three bus. A
masterly disguise, my dear sir, but it doesn't fool me. Clearly you are none
other than my new client, Mr John B. Good.
Ruby I'm not actually. I'm a doctor and I came in my car from Shepherd's
Bush. I'm not disguised, nor is my name Good. It's Watson.
Sherlock Watson? Watson? That rings a bell.
Ruby Well, surely you were told to expect me—Dr Watson?
Sherlock Dr Watson! Of course! I knew at once. The likeness is unmistak-
able. (*He points to the portrait*)
Ruby If that's meant to be flattering——
Sherlock I never flatter. I deal only in facts. Come, take off that skirt.
Ruby What?!
Sherlock You can borrow a pair of my trousers.
Ruby Mr Holmes, I am not a man. I'm a woman.
Sherlock Really, Watson? When did this happen?
Ruby When I was born—as Ruby Watson.
Sherlock Ruby? Ridiculous! Whoever heard of a Watson called Ruby?
Ruby I'm not that kind of Watson, Mr Holmes. I'm a geriatric consultant.
Sherlock Amazing. You look quite young.

Ruby A consultant in geriatrics. And I'm here at the request of your GP, Dr
  Morris——
Sherlock Morris? Moriarty, you mean. The man's a viper. Would you
  believe it, he's trying to get me put away in a nursing home?
Ruby Not put away, Mr Holmes, looked after. And I think he's right. I
  mean, look what happened the last time you tried to get across Baker
  Street in your wheelchair.

She consults a file and he looks rather uncomfortable

  Towed away for causing an obstruction according to the police.
Sherlock Jealousy! The Metropolitan Police have always been jealous of
  me. But I'll show them with my new case. A mysterious matter of a
  disappearing corpse. Fascinating! You shall help me, Watson.
Ruby Mr Holmes, I am not a female reincarnation of your grandfather's
  famous friend. The fact that I am a doctor by the name of Watson is pure
  coincidence.
Sherlock Rubbish. A good detective never believes in coincidence.
Ruby But you are not a—you are not your grandfather, Mr Holmes.
Sherlock Of course I'm not. I'm better. And when our new client arrives——

There is a knock at the door L

  Ah, he has. Let him in, Watson.
Ruby Oh, really. (*Impatiently she moves to open the door*)

John is standing outside. Their eyes meet

Music 10a: A Sudden Shimmer

They gasp simultaneously

Music 10b: Can This Be Love?

John	Got bats in my belfry,
	I'm timid as a mouse.
	You are the cat's pyjamas,
	My gift horse in the mouth.
	I got off my high horse,
	Wormed my way into your life.
	Don't mind being henpecked.
	You bring out the animal in me,
	My little turtle dove.
	So we have to take note,
	No, we're not acting the goat.
John ⎞	Can this be love?
Ruby ⎠	Can this be love?
Ruby	I know I don't feel chicken,
	Anything for a lark.
	You are a snail in the grass,

Your bite's worse than your bark.
Well, I've gone to the dogs,
Made a beeline for your love
And I'm not talking bull.

John ⎫
Ruby ⎭ You bring out the animal in me ... *etc.*

John (*to Ruby*) Gosh, are *you* Sherlock Holmes, Junior?

Sherlock Of course not. I am. She's Watson.

John Dr Watson?

Ruby Yes, but you can call me Ruby.

Sherlock Watson, if you're going to be my assistant, you'll really have to change that name.

Ruby But I'm not going to be your assistant.

John Oh dear.

Ruby Well, maybe—just this once.

Sherlock Good man.

John Hear, hear! That is, good—well, good anyway. Let me explain, I am——

Ruby John B. Good, a solicitor, and you've just come from Lincoln's Inn Fields on a number twenty-three bus.

Sherlock That's my line!

Ruby Yes, I'm sorry, Mr Holmes. But let's hear what John—Mr Good has to say about this disappearing corpse. What exactly is the problem?

John Well, it all began when I went to Enstein Hall.

The Lights fade to Black-out as he continues, letting his voice trail away, and the sound of a clock ticking comes up

I had been called there on behalf of my firm ...

In the Black-out the clock tick gets louder then fades away as the Lights come up

... so what was I to do? What can I do?

The Lights come up to full and the ticking stops

You see my problem, Mr Holmes.

Sherlock No.

Ruby Well, I do and it poses six simple questions. One—what happened to old Mr Enstein's corpse? Two—did Burke and Hare bury empty coffins because they used the bodies to make sausages, bonemeal and wigs? Three—why have they now stopped those sidelines? Four—why have they suddenly moved their undertaking business to Enstein Hall? Five— why is Frank Enstein spending vast sums on electronic equipment? And six—what's the connection between that equipment and the undertaking business?

Sherlock Just what I was going to say. And what are the six simple answers?

Ruby I don't know, but I'm going to find out right now—at Enstein Hall.

John But how will you get in there without arousing suspicion?

Ruby Quite easily. In the one way that won't arouse any suspicion in a funeral parlour.

Black-out. The traverse tabs close

SCENE 3

The Enstein Funeral Parlour

Music 11: Soft Funereal Incidental

The Lights come up revealing a sign that has been flown in, "Enstein Funeral Parlour"

    Burke and Hare enter L *carrying a coffin. They move solemnly across to exit* R *with it*

    After a beat Igor looks through the C *of the tabs. The music fades*

Igor All clear.

    He enters with Mrs Body carrying the prop corpse

Mrs Body How many more times? Why can't we just leave him in one place?

Igor Because the new master keeps using more and more rooms. We don't want to lose old Mr Enstein under a pile of monsters again.

Frank (*off* R) Later, Boris.

Igor Quick!

Mrs Body Where to?

Igor Er—the greenhouse!

    They hurry off L

    Frank and Boris enter R

Boris But you said you'd make me another sort of me.

Frank Sure. And I will—but later.

Boris That's what you always say. It's not fair.

Frank Life isn't, Boris, life isn't.

    Frank exits L

Boris Then it ought to be. If it was there'd be lots of other sorts of me, then I wouldn't have to worry that nobody else seems to want me. I don't know why——

Music 12: I'm Only Monstrous

(*Singing*)   When I'm walking down the street
                    And I think I'm looking very neat,
                    With a sparkle in my eye,
                    I wink at passers-by
                    And raise my hat,
                    But passers-by do—just that!

Nobody wants to talk,
Nobody wants to walk
With me across the park after dark.
They scream when I come near,
I ask you, what's to fear?
I'm only monstrous!

It's prepost'rous,
I'm only monstrous.

And when I think I'm being good,
Sipping daintily on blood,
When I've polished every bolt,
Can't help but taking note
Nobody wants to chat,
The passers-by do—just that!

Nobody seems to care,
Nobody seems to dare ⸲
To come very near to me.
They run away from me,
I wish that they could see
I'm only monstrous!

It's prepost'rous,
I'm only monstrous.

Boris exits L

The traverse tabs open to reveal a desk L, *with Mrs Burkenhare sitting at it,
and a large potted palm* R, *in front of which is a plinth on which Burke and
Hare are putting down their coffin* (*in which Ruby is now hiding*)

Burke There's another one for you, my little darling.

The telephone on the desk rings

Mrs Burkenhare (*on the phone*) The Enstein Funeral Parlour. ... Your
    husband, madam? How sad, but leave everything to us. Mr Burke and Mr
    Hare will be round personally——
Hare But we only just got back——
Mrs Burkenhare Rightaway. What's the address? ... (*She jots it down*)
    Thank you. And believe me, we share in your loss. (*She puts the phone
    down*) Literally. (*Holding out the address*) Here you are, boys, and then
    this evening——
Hare Ah, this evening. Thursday, isn't it? I'm glad you've made some plans.
Mrs Burkenhare I have. You're going out grave robbing.
Burke Again?
Hare That's four nights out of three we've been out. Couldn't we stay in?
Mrs Burkenhare If you do I shall have a headache. So, come along now.

*As they cross to get the address the coffin lid lifts behind them and Ruby peers
out*

Hare You'll work us to death.
Mrs Burkenhare Don't worry, you won't be wasted—not at the rate Frank's using corpses. Off you go.

Ruby lets down the lid as they turn to go

Burke Do you ever get the feeling that she's trying to cut off our conjugals?
Hare Glory be, I hope not!

They exit R

Mrs Burkenhare I think I might have to drop our little tax arrangement. After all, what's the point of two little Willies when I could have——

Frank bursts through the alcove curtains

Frank Eureka!
Mrs Burkenhare Right on cue, but my name's Leucretia, actually.
Frank I know, and Leukie baby, this is it!
Mrs Burkenhare It is? Oh, good!
Frank Yeah! Now I can really do it.
Mrs Burkenhare I was sure you could.
Frank I'm talking about creation!
Mrs Burkenhare So am I—in a way.
Frank Yeah, creation! Regeneration! New life for old! All those experiments, all those failures, all those weeks of waiting—they're over. Look!

Music 13a: New Technology (Dramatic Chord)

The alcove curtains open to reveal a much modernized laboratory, the principal feature of which is a large machine, with dials labelled Parts Assembly, Stitching, Animation, Control and switches marked Head, Torso, Arms, Legs. There are winking lights on the machine and it gives off a burble of electronic noises. Ruby lifts her coffin lid cautiously

My brain-child! OK, Junior, show Poppa what you can do!

Music 13b: Activation

A tremolo which starts as he adjusts each dial and throws each switch, each function being accompanied by a light and a noise

Head! Torso! Arms! Legs! Assembly! Stitching! Animation! (*He pulls a lever*)

There are wild noises ending in a belch. Out pops a Monster

And again! (*He operates a lever*)

Out pops an identical Monster

And again! (*He operates a lever*)

Another Monster

And again!

He continues pulling the lever quicker and quicker to create as many Monsters as desirable

And all with total built-in control!

He pulls another larger lever and immediately the Monsters' movements begin to conform to a pattern, as they march into position

Music 13c: Total Built-in Control

Monsters	Total built-in control, total built-in control, Total built-in control, total built-in control.
Frank	Total! Built-in! Control!
Monsters	Total built-in control.
Frank	Total! Built-in! Control!
Monsters	Total built-in control.
	Personally speaking, There is no rust or squeaking, No need for any maintenance Or old oil can. Total independence, We're in attendance To do most anything a human can!
Frank	Do most anything a human can! Total! Built-in! Control!
Monsters	Total built-in control.
Frank	Total! Built-in! Control!
Monsters	Total built-in control.
	We're at your right hand, What is your command? Give us your signal For total built-in, built-in control, Total built-in, built-in control.
Frank **Monsters** }	Total built-in, built-in control!

Frank adjusts some controls and the Monsters go into a little of the pas de quatre *from "Swan Lake"; he readjusts and they break into a Tiller Girls routine; he readjusts again and they start to tap dance. All this is observed by Ruby, who emerges from the coffin and hides behind the potted palm to get a better look*

Monsters Total built-in control, total built-in control,
Total built-in control, total built-in control,
Total built-in control, total built-in control,
Total built-in control, total built-in control,
Total built-in control, total built-in control.

We don't need any teaching,
We'll not submit to leeching,
No need for any programmes,
We're all OK.
Total independence,
Just you say a sentence
We'll do just as you want and straightaway!
Do just as you want and straightaway!

Frank Total!
Built-in!
Control!

Monsters Total built-in control.

Frank Total!
Built-in!
Control!

Monsters Total built-in control.

We're at your right hand,
What is your command?
Give us your signal
For total built-in, built-in control——

Frank Total built-in, built-in control——

All Total built-in, built-in control!
Total!
Built-in!
Built-in!
Control!
Total!
Built-in!
Built-in!
Control!
Total built-in control, total built-in control ... *etc.*

Continuing until Frank marches the Monsters off at the end of the number

The Monsters exit

Mrs Burkenhare Frank, it's wonderful!
Ruby It's terrible!
Mrs Burkenhare It's a miracle!
Ruby It's a nightmare!
Mrs Burkenhare There's no stopping us now!
Ruby There must be!

Mrs Burkenhare We'll run the country!
Frank The country? Why not Europe?
Frank
}(*together*) The world!
Mrs Burkenhare
Frank And we'll do it efficiently, scientifically——
Mrs Burkenhare And very profitably!
Frank And all out of waste. What's more, my baby here gives a perfect model every time. (*He pulls the lever*)

Out comes a four-legged, no-armed, no-headed Monster

Oh no! (*He reverses the lever*)

The Monster retreats into the machine

Igor!

A leg is thrown on from L, *swiftly followed by another leg, then an irate Igor carrying a third leg that he throws down*

Igor Legs! I'm sick of 'em! Every day I go down to the stockroom and what do I find? Legs! I'm up to my neck in legs! Something'll have to be done.
Frank Then do it! You're in charge of the stock.
Igor But the stock's all legs!
Frank Well, it shouldn't be.

Burke and Hare enter R

Igor I know, but don't blame me, blame them!
Burke
}(*together*) What for!
Hare
Igor Legs!
Burke What's wrong with our legs?
Igor There's too many of 'em.
Hare (*looking down*) Seems the right number to me.
Frank Not your legs, dead legs. Look, you're in charge of supply, so how come you're only supplying legs?
Burke Graves.
Frank What?
Burke Very dark in the graves. You can't tell what you're getting at all.
Frank I don't want excuses, I want corpses. Whole corpses.
Burke Don't get on to us, we're always carting coffins or digging up graves. There's only so many hours in the day, you know.
Hare Yes, and we're already working twenty-five of them.
Igor Looking for more legs, I suppose.
Burke If you can't sort out what we give you——
Igor You only give me legs! Fat lot of sorting out there. Only left or right.
Burke And what about the two corpses we've brought in today—whole corpses?
Hare The widow-woman's husband we've just fetched has nothing missing.
Burke Nor's that darling one over there. Have you had a look at her?

Consternation from Ruby as he points at her coffin

Frank Never mind her, she's just one corpse.

Ruby shows relief

Hare Ah, but what a one. There's more than legs to her. Just look now.

Ruby cringes back into the potted palm in alarm as he crosses to lift the lid

Frank No!

Hare reluctantly moves away, to Ruby's great relief

I'm not interested in just one corpse, or two corpses, I want two hundred—two thousand! All my plans rely on corpses. Landsakes! Surely the world's not short of corpses?

Mrs Burkenhare Of course not. There's plenty of them around. They're just not dead yet.

Frank What are they hanging around for? I need them! How can people be so selfish?

Mrs Burkenhare Well, it's up to us to help them. And I've just thought, I know exactly how we can. People will come flocking—to be corpses.

Burke Sounds like a lot of work for us.

Hare Yes, it'll be murder.

Mrs Burkenhare Oh no, that's the beauty of it. It'll be—well, voluntary. They'll do it for the fun of the thing.

Frank What, become corpses?

Mrs Burkenhare Yes. All we need are the right premises, and then——

Loud crashing and bangings off L, *like a pile of falling logs, and shrieks from Mrs Body, off*

All (*except Igor and Ruby*) What's that?

Igor The legs!

Mrs Body (*muffled, off* L) Help!

Igor Mrs Body! I left her with the legs!

All except Ruby run off L

Ruby (*emerging*) This is awful! It's worse than we thought. Somehow we must stop them.

Boris enters L

Well, at least they don't know that we know about their plans. In fact, they don't know about us at all. (*She starts to move* R)

Boris Stop!

She spins round, sees Boris and is horrified

I want you!

She remains rooted to the spot as he moves ponderously and with seeming menace towards her

You're a pretty monster.

Ruby Wh-what?

Boris You're the prettiest monster I've met.

Ruby Oh, I see, you think I'm——

Boris Just what I've always wanted, the other sort of me. I think you've got lovely differences. Can you walk like me, though? (*He demonstrates his walk*)

Ruby Oh, er—of course! (*She copies his walk*)

Boris Cor, smashing! (*He moves close to her*) Here, do you know what monsters do when they get together?

Ruby No.

Boris Pity. Neither do I. I'm having a burst of electricity soon. Would you like one too? P'raps they could plug us in together.

Ruby Oh, no! Because I—er—I'm plugged in with somebody else.

Boris Some *body*? I thought they only plugged in monsters.

Ruby That's what I meant. Some monster else.

Boris Else? I don't know Else. But isn't Else another other sort?

Ruby Not my else. My else is one of your sort.

Boris Funny sort of my sort.

Ruby He's not. He's tall and handsome and strong and—just like a film star.

Boris So was I—once. I'd still like to plug in with you.

Ruby Sorry, you can't. I've told you, I'm plugging steady.

Boris You didn't. You said you was plugging Else.

Ruby Yes, I'm plugging steady with else.

Boris Cor! Can't I join in too then?

Ruby What? Oh, no! Certainly not! Anyway, I must go now——

Boris (*stopping her*) What for?

Ruby A walk.

Boris Ah, practising, eh?

Ruby Practising? Oh yes, practising.

Ruby monster-walks off R

Boris Cor! Lovely little mover. She must have gone to meet Else. Or Steady. What have they got that I haven't? Sometimes I think I've got something missing. But somehow——

Music 14: There Must Be a Way

The Lights fade to a Spot on Boris and the traverse tabs close. As Boris sings, the alcove curtains are closed and the desk, coffin, potted palm, doors etc. are struck. Burke, Hare, Sherlock, Mrs Burkenhare, Igor, Mrs Body, Frank, John and Ruby enter and take up their positions behind the traverse tabs

(*Singing*) There must be a way
For me to get hold of you,
My little monster.
There must be a way
To find another kind of me.

You're so fiendish,
You're so horrible,

You're so grotesque,
It is wonderful.
There must be a way
For me to get hold of you,
For me to get hold of you,
For me to get hold of you.

Monsters enter L *and* R

Boris   ⎫ If there's a way,
Monsters ⎭ We'll find it.
                If it cuts up rough,
                We'll grind it,
                Throw ourselves into the fray,
                Get on our knees and pray.
                If there's a way
                We're gonna find it,
                We're gonna find it.

The traverse tabs open

Monsters We are the way,
                The future is ours, you'll see.
                We are the way,
                The future is ours, you'll see.
                (*Continue, repeating under all the following*)
Boris   There must be a way
                For me to get hold of you,
                My little monster.
                There must be a way
                To find another kind of me.
                (*Continue, repeating under all the following*)

Lights come up in various areas to illuminate each succeeding contributor

Burke ⎫ The only way for us to go
Hare ⎭ Is to see your blood flowing
                Nice 'n' sleazy.
                (*Continue, repeating under all the following*)
Sherlock I know that there's a way
                To be a detective and be
                Respected.
                (*Continue, repeating under all the following*)
Mrs Burkenhare   I know just the way
                To seduce so that he will be
                Affected.
                (*Continue, repeating under all the following*)
Igor   ⎫ And with the master's corpse we'll go
Mrs Body ⎭ Seeking high and seeking low
                Where to save him.
                (*Continue, repeating under all the following*)

Frank   I know just the way
For all the people to see
My monsters.
(*Continue, repeating under the following*)

Ruby ⎫   And we'll find a way
John ⎭   To stop him from ruling the world,
The monster!
We'll find a way,
We'll save it you'll see.
(*Repeat*)

All   We are the way,
The future is ours, you'll see.
We are the way,
The future is ours, you'll see.
We are the way,
The future is ours, you'll see.

CURTAIN

ACT II

Scene 1

Suspended upstage is a sign saying "Enstein Enterprises". There are desks with typewriters on one side and tables with telephones on the other

As the Curtain *rises rhythmic typing is heard, intertwined with the rhythm of telephones ringing. Lady Monsters typing and Lady Monsters answering the telephones are discovered and so are Igor, Mrs Body and Mrs Burkenhare. Male Monsters, as clerks, enter, exit and move between the groups of Lady Monsters with bundles of orders, etc.*

Music 15: Business Is Big

All	Business is big,
	It's gigantic,
	That's why we get
	Ever so frantic,
	Working our fingers to the bone,
	Ringing of the phone—
	Business is good,
	Business is big!
Mrs Burkenhare	Business is good,
	It's terrific!
	It could never
	Be soporific,
	All the monsters that we make
	Will keep us wide awake—
	Business is good,
	Business is big!
Monsters	Business is grand,
	It is super,
	In fact you can
	Add on a duper!
	Yes, we are really going to win,
	Orders keep coming in—
	Business is good,
	Business is big!
All	We don't know the figure,
	But it's getting bigger
	And if we're found out

We don't give a fig;
Don't know the reason,
Perhaps it's the season,
What ever it is
It's good for the biz.

Business is ace,
It's exciting;
In order books
We're always writing;
As long as someone always dies
We will have supplies—
Business is ace,
Business is big!

Mrs Body   Business is great,
It's amazing!
No time for sleep
Or lazing.
All day long we never stop,
Orders for our stock—
Business is great,
Business is big!

Igor   Business is brill',
It's fantastic!
We're at full stretch,
Like elastic.
The likes of this I've never known,
Demand for skin and bone—
Business is brill'—
Business is big!

All   We don't know the figure . . . *etc.—and repeat*

Frank enters, holding a remote control unit

Frank OK, you lot, take five. (*He jabs some buttons on the unit*)

All the Monsters turn and march off

Igor
Mrs Body } (*together*) Ooh!

Mrs Burkenhare That's handy.

Frank Yeah, remote control. I figured we didn't need to keep going to the machine every time. So, how's tricks?

Mrs Burkenhare Terrific! Orders from the Army——

Igor The Navy——

Mrs Body The Air Force——

Igor And the TUC.

Frank Great. And the stocks?

Mrs Body Plenty. Mrs Burkenhare's new idea keeps 'em rolling in.

The telephone rings, Mrs Burkenhare answers it

Mrs Burkenhare Enstein Enterprises? . . . Oh, certainly, madam (*or sir*). All models can be programmed to say or do just whatever you want. . . . I see. . . . You'd like them delivered right away, six hundred and forty-nine of them? . . . To number ten—which street? . . . Oh, that number ten. And send the invoice to number eleven. Of course. . . . Not at all. Thank you, madam (*or sir*).

Frank Leukie baby, was that who I think it was?

Mrs Burkenhare It certainly was.

Frank Then this is our chance. Once we get in there we can really run the country.

Mrs Burkenhare And we'll be rich, really rich!

Igor We won't.

Mrs Burkenhare Why not?

Igor Six hundred and forty-nine monsters, that's why not. Our stocks are good, but not that good.

Mrs Burkenhare But this is one opportunity we can't afford to miss. Somehow my two Willies must increase their turnover at the new premises.

Frank All they need is a whole lot of suckers with more curiosity than sense. You know, sensation seeking idiots like—like——

Mrs Body American tourists?

Frank Atta girl, Beattie baby, American tourists! I'll go make sure the boys can handle this, you go grab yourself a coach party or two.

Frank exits R *with the remote control unit*

Mrs Burkenhare A coach party or two? Well, why not?

Mrs Burkenhare exits L

Igor You know what this means, don't you? More work. You can hardly move in here for monsters as it is. Oh, the old master would turn in his grave.

Mrs Body What grave?

Igor Well, the grave he'd be in if we dared leave him there long enough to be in it. (*He sighs*) Ah, things were different in his day.

Mrs Body (*sighing*) Um, none of this production line stuff then.

Igor No, all bespoke work. Like Boris. Ah——

Music 16: Business Was Small

(*Singing*)   Business was small,
                     It was teeny;
                     In fact I'd say
                     It was weeny,
                     But just the size for having fun,
                     Our work was quickly done—
                     We had quite a ball!
                     Business was small.

Mrs Body	Business was small,
	It was midget,
	About so big—(*She indicates with thumb and finger*)
Igor	Like this digit. (*He holds up his little finger*)
Mrs Body	Plenty of time to skive and shirk,
	For there wasn't any work—
	No need to walk tall,
	Business was small.

Everything smaller,
Nothing was taller,
Even our Boris
Has grown since then.
Lived on a shoe-string,
And that's why we now sing
Of wonderful days
When business was small.

Mrs Body	Business was small,
	It was tiny.
Igor	We didn't complain
	Or get whiney.

Mrs Body }	You'd need a magnifying glass
Igor }	To see the work we'd pass,
	Or see it at all!
	Business was small.

Everything smaller ... *etc.*

The traverse tabs close

SCENE 2

Outside Enstein Hall

Sherlock (*off* L) Very well, officer. I'm moving as quickly as I can.

He enters in his wheelchair, heavily disguised as a match-seller

Tcha! Officious busybody. I'd say it was professional jealousy, only of course he can't see through my masterly disguise. Now, low profile surveillance, that's the thing. (*He puts on a pair of dark glasses*) Hm, tricky. Still, as long as I'm natural. (*Bawling*) MATCHES! MATCHES! LOVELY FRESH MATCHES! GET YOUR MATCHES HERE!

Frank enters R

No good. Nobody there.
Frank What's that?
Sherlock Ah, there is, good. Buy a box of matches, sir.
Frank What for? I've got a lighter.
Sherlock Mean so and so.

Ruby and John dash on R

Ruby ⎫
John ⎰ (*together*) Mr Holmes!

Sherlock Yes? I mean, no. I'm not me.

Ruby Mr Holmes, this is no time for games.

Sherlock Games!

Ruby Do you know who that was?

Sherlock No, can't see a thing through these.

John That was Enstein.

Sherlock Who?

Ruby Frank Enstein. Our chief suspect.

Sherlock Yes, I thought he was suspicious the way he didn't want any matches. Where's he going?

Ruby We don't know, but we intend to find out. Come on, Johnnie!

John Rather!

They run off L

Sherlock Wait! You need masterly disguises! Hopeless. Amateurs. Not like me.

Music 17: Elementary

(*Singing*)   I have great affection
For what I call detection,
Murderers and forgers are my quest,
Sometimes I act on tips
And then I match my wits,
Slowly sleuthing, putting theories to the test.

But anyone who is a party
To the likes of Moriarty
Will find themselves securely locked in jail,
Whether he's a burglar,
Or some cold-blooded murd'rer,
In the strongest terms I will object to bail.

I'll tell you how they died,
It's as easy as pie;
Or who's on the take,
It's a piece of cake,
To me they're complement'ry,
For to me ... it's element'ry!

I'm strong for I played rugger,
So woe betide the mugger
Ev'ry football hooligan I will boot!
I'll know if you're unruly,
For I have got my stoolie
Who'll sing, whilst I accomp'ny with your loot.

My great detective prowess
Is due to thinking powers
Called upon when smoking on my pipe.
It may create a stink,
But smoking helps me think
And locate the hiding place of what you swipe.

I'll tell you how they died . . . *etc.*

Now if you've told a whopper
A very cunning copper
In questioning I will turn out to be,
For if you are a fraud
'Tis a matter of accord
That through your web of lies I will surely see.

I can get very fiery
When making an enquiry,
So watch out, Enstein, I know of your plan.
It really is amazing,
You may think I'm lazing,
But in the end I always get my man!

I'll tell you how they died . . . *etc.—and repeat*

Ruby and John run on L

(*Speaking*)   My dear Watson,
                My dear Watson,
(*Singing*)   It's elementary!
Did someone say encore?
Ruby No! Anyway there isn't time.
John No, because we've found what we've been looking for all these weeks.
Sherlock Really? What have we been looking for all these weeks?
John ⎫
Ruby ⎭ (*together*) Enstein's new premises!
Ruby And they're called, "The Dungeon of Death"!

Black-out. The traverse tabs open

SCENE 3

The Dungeon of Death

A suitably macabre setting, dimly lit to open, with a sign hanging down reading—"Dungeon of Death. Panorama of Execution through the Ages". The shadow of a noose and gallows is thrown on from R *and upstage from* R *to* L *there is an electric chair, an execution block with a huge axe and a low screen, behind which we see the top of a guillotine. In front of the screen is a large basket, above which is a small chute set into the screen. There is an entrance* R, *just upstage of which is a bell-push labelled—"FIRING SQUAD", and a door* L, *marked "WAY OUT"*

Music 18a: Spooky Incidental

The music plays for a few moments then suddenly the Lights come up
Burke and Hare leap on

Music 18b: Gaily, Daily, Dealing Out Death

Burke }   Gaily, daily, dealing out death,
Hare   Wotta lot we got,
We're all short of breath.
Insanely, humanely, we'll do our best,
It's over in a trice,
They are put to rest.

They can grope at the rope,
They can mope down the slope,
But when all is done and said
Everyone will end up dead;
It's the end,
There's no hope!
It's the end,
There's no hope!

Burke   It's a pleasure,
You're a treasure,
We give new meaning
To government cuts.

Hare   At our leisure
We will measure
You for the chopping block
With no ifs or buts.

Burke }   It's—
Hare   Gaily, daily, dealing out death ... *etc.*

They can grope at the rope ... *etc.*

Hare   You're invited,
We're excited,
For here in the Dungeon
We have got it made.

Burke   We're delighted
You have sighted
Our friend the chopping block
With its cold, sharp blade.
Our blade—

Hare   It's sharp!
Burke   Oh, sharp!

Burke }   Let's go!
Hare

Instrumental

Burke	Gaily!	**Hare**	It's the end,
			There's no hope!
	Daily!		It's the end,
			There's no hope!
	Gaily!		It's the end,
			There's no hope!
	Daily!		It's the end,
			There's no hope!
	Gaily!		It's the end,
			There's no hope!
	Daily!		It's the end,
			There's no hope!

Burke ⎫ It's the end,
Hare ⎭ There's no hope!
It's the end,
There's no hope!

Burke Ah, there's nothing like job satisfaction.

Hare Yes, to be sure. And I never did like the graves. All those worms in my wellies.

Boris (*off* R) Head in, head out. Head in, head out. Head in—one, two, three, jump!

There is a loud crash off R

Burke ⎫ (*together*) Boris!
Hare ⎭

Boris enters R *with a noose round his neck and the broken end of the rope hanging free*

Burke What d'ye think you're doing?

Boris Just hanging around.

Burke Well, you've broken the gallows. The trouble is we've so many customers this stuff's getting overworked.

Hare Then let's test the lot. (*He sits in the electric chair*) Right, switch on.

Burke is about to do so, then stops

Burke Willie, have you thought this through?

Hare I have. If it doesn't work I'll be all right, and if it does—(*He pauses, then rises*) Maybe you'd better test it, Willie.

Boris Have you got another one of these I can break?

Burke No, but you can try breaking this.

He pushes Boris into the electric chair

Right!

Hare switches on the chair. Flashing tube lights and crackling noises. Boris goes rigid

Hare Yes, that's working. (*He switches the chair off*)

Burke Maybe a bit too well.
Boris (*relaxing*) I liked that. Can I have another go?
Burke Not now, Boris, we've work to do. Just get on the block.

Boris sits on the block

No, no, don't sit on it. Kneel down and put your head on it.
Boris (*doing so*) Why?
Burke You'll see.
Hare (*struggling with the axe*) Maybe. Glory be, no wonder the arms fell off
   the creature that does this.

*He brings the axe down on Boris's neck. (Prop axe with the head carved out of
thick foam rubber) The axe appears to bounce up with added force, narrowly
missing Burke as it swings back*

Burke Mind out!
Hare It's not my fault. It's blunt.
Boris (*rising, a bit lop-sided*) I didn't like that. Given me a crick, that has.
Burke (*pushing him behind the guillotine screen*) Don't worry, put your head
   here and it'll disappear entirely.

The guillotine blade descends with a sickening thud then immediately rises

Boris Ow!
Hare What's the matter? Are you dead?
Boris (*re-emerging*) No, but you've dented my steel neck.

   He exits huffily L

Burke A steel neck?
Hare Oh, heck.
Burke Let's try the Firing Squad. (*He pushes the "FIRING SQUAD"
   button*)

*An arrow descends R, pointing downwards. On it is written "CUSTOMER
STAND HERE"*

*A troop of Monsters as the Firing Squad in military uniforms and bearing
rifles, marches in L and halts C. They are led by an Officer Monster with a
sword, which he raises as he steps forward*

Officer Monster Aim!

The Squad bring up their rifles

(*Lowering his sword*) Fire!

*The Squad suddenly swings round to face L. Burke and Hare drop to the
ground as the Squad fires*

   They then march off L over the prone pair and the arrow is flown out

Burke I wish that wouldn't happen every time.

   Frank hurries on R

Frank Hey, Willies, where are you? (*He almost trips over them*) Fellers, this is no time for lying down on the job, we've got a rush order on. Any minute now there'll be customers here in their hundreds.

Burke and Hare rise

Burke Hundreds? We like to let them in one at a time so's they can have a nice peaceful death on their own.

Hare Yes, we don't want them to feel they're just one of a crowd.

Frank That's very thoughtful of you boys, but we need corpses and we need them fast. And this is just one part of the operation—there's all the sorting and reassembly, that's what takes the time.

Hare Then why don't you just use them as they are?

Frank Don't be ridiculous, use them as they are! That's ... That's brilliant! Of course, simply reanimation! I'll go programme it right away. Willie babe, you're a genius!

Frank rushes off R

Hare Did you hear that?

Burke I did, but don't worry. He must have thought he was talking to me.

They exit L, Hare dragging with him the axe

Igor and Mrs Body enter R, she pushing the wheelbarrow with the prop corpse in it

Mrs Body Oh my poor feet. Pity we couldn't have brought him on the bus.

Igor I know, but they don't seem to like wheelbarrows on buses. Well now, that big fridge should be just the place for him. Wheel him in.

He opens the "WAY OUT" door, revealing that on its other side it is constructed like a fridge door. Some dry ice rolls out

Mrs Body What? In there? With my twinges? Not likely. I'm going to rest before this big rush starts.

Mrs Body exits L

Igor shrugs and pushes the wheelbarrow and corpse into the fridge

Igor You'll like it here, sir. Should be lots of company for you soon. (*He reappears without the wheelbarrow*) You might even be able to stay there for the rest of your life. (*He shuts the fridge door*) Er—death.

After a slight pause, Ruby and John enter R stealthily, followed by Sherlock in his wheelchair which is squeaking loudly

Ruby
John } (*together*) Ssh!

Ruby You might have oiled that, Mr Holmes.

Sherlock It doesn't make any difference, Watson. It always creaks when it creeps. (*He looks around*) Hm, interesting place and with just one look I can immediately deduce the kind of people we're dealing with.

Ruby Me too.

John And me.

Sherlock Oh. Really? Hm—good. Then we're agreed—they're specialist antique thieves.

Ruby
John } (*together*) Ye—what!?

Sherlock Ah, so you hadn't realized that. Well, it takes a trained mind. But they've made one mistake. You can't buy this sort of stuff. Therefore, they must have stolen it. We'll get them for that, Watson.

Ruby Mr Holmes, it's nothing to do with stolen goods. Can't you see, this place is a do-it-yourself murder parlour? Nobody leaves here alive.

Sherlock Nonsense, of course they do. Otherwise, why have a way out?

John I don't know, but—— (*He opens the fridge door*) Hey, it's not a way out, it's a fridge. And a jolly big fridge.

Ruby A fridge? Of course! When the customers are dead they're——

John They're corpses!

Ruby They store them there!

Sherlock Rubbish!

John They do, there's one there already.

Ruby (*sitting back on the electric chair*) My God!

Sherlock Doubtless a waxwork. Let us investigate.

He disappears with John into the fridge. Ruby realizes the nature of her chair and hastily rises

Igor (*off* L) All right, I'll open in five minutes.

Ruby crouches R of the chair

Igor enters wearing a cap and doing up a commissionaire's coat

The things I have to do nowadays. (*He notices the fridge door is open*) I thought I shut that.

He shuts it and Ruby creeps behind the chair to L of it as he crosses R

Might put the customers off if they see how they end up.

Igor exits R

Ruby is about to open the fridge

Burke and Hare enter L. Hare has the axe

Ruby steps back and inadvertently collapses into the electric chair, where she sits rigid

Hare Ah, you could shave yourself with it now—if you could get it up to your face. (*He puts it beside block*) Perhaps Mrs Body can sew the arms back on the monster, though.

Burke (*noticing Ruby*) Will you look at that now? Five minutes he said and he's let one in already.

Hare Well, at least she's done the right thing by herself.

They lift her, still holding herself rigid, and carry her towards the fridge

Here, haven't we had her before.

Burke We can't have. Nobody dies twice.

They are startled by a loud knocking from behind the door and drop Ruby

Hare They do if they live twice! They're coming back from the dead, Willie!
Burke They can't be, we emptied it, remember? It must be that old fool Igor shut himself in.
Hare Ah, of course. (*He opens the door*) Come on out, you old eejit.

Sherlock shivers out with his deerstalker earflaps down

Burke |
Hare | (*together*) Wrong eejit!

They draw pistols as John, with his coat collar up and pushing the wheelbarrow with the corpse also shivers out

Freeze!
John W-w-we are.
Burke What are you doing there? Customers aren't supposed to go there.
Hare Well, not to begin with.
Sherlock W-w-we're not c-c-customers. W-w-we are——
John Shut up!

Ruby starts to crawl over to the axe

Burke We know you. You're that lawyer! Spying on us, eh? Who's this?
John Oh—er—nobody important.
Sherlock Not important? Me? The world's greatest detective, Sherlock Holmes Junior!
Burke You'll soon be meeting Senior, then. Who's the third one?
Sherlock Watson.

Ruby has reached the axe and is desperately trying to lift it

Hare What's he doing in a wheelbarrow?
Sherlock Eh? Oh, that's not Watson. Watson's behind you.

Burke and Hare swing round just as Boris enters L and John says—

John You fool!

Ruby sees Boris and screams, dropping the axe, while John charges Burke and Hare with the wheelchair, Sherlock with feet outstretched. Hare falls on to the switch as Burke staggers back into the electric chair. He leaps up and Hare switches it off

Boris Hullo. Want some help? (*He picks up the axe with ease*)
Ruby Yes, get them!
Boris Right.

Whirling the axe round his head he goes for John and Sherlock with it, but misses because they duck. John pushes Sherlock to R beside the "FIRING SQUAD" button

Ruby Not that them! That them!

Boris Oh, right.

He chases Burke and Hare in a clockwise circle

John Let's get out of here!
Ruby The evidence! Get the corpse!

John rushes over to grab the wheelbarrow and pulls it to R. *Burke and Hare break away to* L, *but Hare trips and falls behind the guillotine screen. Burke desperately tries to pull him away*

Burke Willie!

The blade descends. Hare re-emerges as it rises

Hare Missed.
John Right, come on!

Before Ruby can move to push the wheelchair, Boris is beside her

Boris No. I want you.

He throws her over his shoulder in a fireman's lift. John moves in to him

John I say—er—look, old chap, she's——
Boris She's mine.

   He shoves John upstage to Sherlock and exits R, *with a loudly protesting Ruby ineffectually pummelling his back*

Burke ⎫
Hare ⎭ (*together levelling their pistols*) Hands up!

John and Sherlock put their hands up sharply, Sherlock inadvertently knocking the "FIRING SQUAD" button. The arrow descends over them

Burke Now we've got you!

   The Firing Squad enter, kicking Burke and Hare over and trampling over them

John and Sherlock look relieved at the diversion

Officer Monster (*raising his sword*) Aim!

John and Sherlock look less relieved as the Squad do so. Burke and Hare, rather befuddled, start to rise

   (*Lowering his sword*) Fire!

The Squad swings round as before and Burke and Hare drop down just in time as they fire

   The Squad marches off over Burke and Hare and the arrow is flown out

John propels Sherlock to the exit R

Sherlock Aren't we going to arrest them?
John No!

He shoves him off R, *then follows with the wheelbarrow*

Burke and Hare stagger up

Burke After them!

As they run R *they are met by a party of American Tourists entering there*

Tourists Gee, ain't this really something?

Music 19: Put Your Head Upon the Block

During the number the Tourists try out the electric chair and the guillotine for themselves. As the blade descends and rises heads are dropped down the chute into the basket. Burke and Hare, with help later from Igor and Mrs Body, remove the ensuing corpses to the fridge

Male **Tourists**	See the lovely guillotine, Honey, ain't it really cute? A head rollin' down the chute.
Female **Tourists**	Look here, Hiram, it's surprisin', Your head will soon be rollin'.
Burke⎫ **Hare** ⎭	Put your head upon the block, we'll chop it off. Put your head upon the block, we'll chop it off.
Tourists	No such wonderful things back home, A revelation! No such wonders in Idaho, Decapitation!
Burke⎫ **Hare** ⎭	Now at our work we're so professional, The bumping-off is so processional. Tourists to the right and left of us Find their way to us without a fuss. Yes, they find their way to us without a fuss. You want a corpse? Then we can cater, A headless one is much safer. Two, four, six, eight, Time for you to Time for you to terminate. Yes, it's time for you to terminate.
Tourists	Gee whizz, honey, it's so wonderful! Oh so quaint!
Burke⎫ **Hare** ⎭	Put your head upon the block.
Tourists	Guillotine without a trial, Well, it's done with so much style.
Burke⎫ **Hare** ⎭	Put your head upon the block, we'll chop it off. Put your head upon the block, we'll chop it off.
Tourists	No such wonderful things back home, A revelation! No such wonders in Idaho, Decapitation!

Burke Put your head upon the block, we'll chop it off.
Hare   Put your head upon the block, we'll chop it off.

Igor and Mrs Body enter R, *moving to the electric chair*

Igor   ⎫ Put your seat upon the seat, we'll turn you on.
Mrs Body ⎭ Put your seat upon the seat, we'll turn you on.
Hare   Put your neck beneath the blade, we'll cut you short.
               Put your neck beneath the blade, we'll cut you short.
Burke   Put your head ... *etc* ⎫ 12 TIMES   **Tourists** Gee whizz, it's   ⎫ 6 TIMES
Igor   ⎫ Put your seat ... *etc* ⎬   quaint,   ⎬
Mrs Body ⎭   ⎪   Can't wait to tell my   ⎪
Hare   Put your neck ... *etc* ⎭   friends back home.   ⎭
Burke
Hare   ⎫ Put your head upon the block, we'll chop it off.
Igor   ⎬ Put your head upon the block, we'll chop it off.
Mrs Body ⎭

Some remaining Tourists press the "FIRING SQUAD" button and the arrow descends over them

The Squad enters

Officer Monster (*raising his sword*) Aim!

As the Squad raise their rifles Burke and Hare drop to the ground L

Igor and Mrs Body run off R

The Tourists scream and run to L

Officer Monster (*lowering his sword*) Fire!

The Squad swings round and annihilates the remaining Tourists

Hare Well, at least you can rely on them to be contrary. Now they'll march over us.

But the Squad unexpectedly about turns and marches off R

That's funny.
Burke It's not. They're in the street! After them!

Music 20: Chase Incidental

The chase music continues into the next scene

As Burke and Hare run off R—

Black-out, and the traverse tabs close

SCENE 4

A Street

The Lights come up DS. *A sign hangs down* C *saying, "A STREET"*

 Boris enters L, *with Ruby still over his shoulder*

Ruby Put me down! Put me down!
Boris No. He never made me one so I'll keep you.
Ruby What for? What are you going to do with me?
Boris I'm going to—I'm going to——
Ruby Yes?
Boris I still haven't found out.

 He lumbers off R *with her*

 Sherlock enters L *in his wheelchair. As he reaches* C *John runs on* L *with the wheelbarrow and corpse, overtaking him*

Sherlock Wait for me!
John (*stopping and turning and seeing something off* L) No!

 He bolts off R. *Sherlock looks off* L, *registers and wheels himself off* R *as quickly as he can*

 The Firing Squad march on L *and continue off* R

 As they disappear Burke and Hare, rather puffed, enter L

Hare Oi! Wait! Stop!
Burke That's no good. You've got to give them proper orders like—Halt! (*Obviously they do not*) Halt, I said. Mark time, then.
Hare About turn!
Burke You fool, they have!

 They drop to the ground as the Squad marches on R *with their rifles raised*

Hare Don't worry. As you were, at the double!

 The Squad about turns and runs off R

Burke Now look what you've done. And four-minute milers every one of them. Come on!

 They run off R. *A strobe lantern starts as Boris and Ruby move across from* L *to* R, *followed by John pushing Sherlock, who is pushing the wheelbarrow from his wheelchair. They are followed by the Firing Squad, then Burke and Hare, who collapse exhausted in* C. *The strobe and the music stop*

 Igor and Mrs Body enter L

Igor Somewhere, he must be somewhere. Ah. (*Deliberately casual*) Either of you seen a corpse?
Burke Hundreds. Which particular one?
Mrs Body A very particular one. But he's not where we left him.
Burke And where was that?
Igor Originally, in the larder——
Mrs Body Then in the box-room——
Igor The outside loo——

Mrs Body The broom cupboard——
Igor The greenhouse——
Mrs Body And, last of all, in that big fridge.
Hare He sounds very active for a corpse. Are you sure he was dead?
Burke We've no time for one corpse, dead or alive. With that Firing Squad
  loose the streets could be littered with corpses. And worse than that, the
  Dungeon was crawling with spies.
Igor Spies!
Mrs Body What spies?
Burke That young lawyer chap for one.
Mrs Body Not young Mr Good?
Burke The very same.
Hare And that old geezer in a wheelchair who claimed he was Sherlock
  Holmes's grandfather.
Burke No, no, grandson. And there was that Watson woman Boris picked
  up—literally.
Hare Not to mention the other old party in a wheelbarrow.
Igor   ⎫
Mrs Body ⎬ (*together*) A wheelbarrow!
Hare Yes, very quiet he was.
Igor I'm not surprised.
Burke But they know all about everything. You'd better warn them at
  Enstein Hall while we try to find the Firing Squad.
Mrs Body That shouldn't take long.
Burke Why not?
Mrs Body They're just coming.

Burke and Hare look off R

Burke Down!

*He and Hare and Igor flatten themselves, then grab Mrs Body and pull her
down*

Mrs Body Careful! Me twinges!

The Firing Squad run on R, *over them and off* L

Me twinges! Me twinges! Me—ooh!

Burke and Hare jump up; Igor and Mrs Body rise more slowly

Burke Now's our chance!

He and Hare start to run off L

Igor Wait! Where's the one in a wheelbarrow?
Hare With the young lawyer.

They exit L

Igor The old master in the hands of the law! He won't like that.
Mrs Body Neither will you if we don't hurry and warn Mr Enstein.
Igor Oh, very well. We'll take it in turns to run. You first.

Mrs Body runs a few steps to R, *with a protesting cry at each step, then stops*

Mrs Body Ooh, me twinges! Your turn.

Igor runs slowly off R *and she walks off after him*

The street sign C *is flown out and another sign, "FURTHER ALONG THE STREET", is flown in* LC

John enters L, *pushing the wheelbarrow and corpse*

John Mr Holmes! Mr Holmes! Well, I suppose he'll catch up eventually. Not that he'll be much use when he does. But we must find some way to rescue Ruby.

The introduction to Music 21 starts

Gosh, when I think of it! In the hands of that—that fiend in fiendish form! Shall I ever see my love again?

Music 21: Shall I Ever See My Love Again

(*Singing*)   Well, I've seen the Eiffel Tower
And I've spent more than an hour
Looking at the Pyramids.
Seen Niagara Falls;
It was such a mortal blow
When I went to Jericho
To see the ice cream sold
Was sold by Walls.

A sign is flown in RC, *"ROUND THE CORNER" as Boris enters* R, *with Ruby*

Ruby   Well, I've been to Lenin's tomb
And I've been in Shakespeare's room,
Caught a glimpse of Taj Mahal,
London in the rain;
It was such a mortal blow
When to Paris I did go
While walking by the river
I nearly went in Seine.

John \
Ruby /   I've seen most ev'rything,
A president, a king;
Things that gave me pleasure,
Things that gave me pain,
But every place I've been,
And everything I've seen,
The thing that bothers me
Is
Shall I ever see my love again?

John   Oh, Ruby!

Ruby	Oh, John!
John ⎱ **Ruby** ⎰	Oh, lover!
	Yeah, I've seen ev'rything,
	A president, a king . . . *etc.*
John	Oh, Ruby!
Ruby	Oh, John!
John ⎱ **Ruby** ⎰	Go on!
	I love you,
	Yes, I really do.
	I love you,
	Yes, I really do.

Boris yanks Ruby off R *and the* RC *sign is flown out*

Sherlock enters L

Sherlock Ah, there you are at last. I've got a plan.

John So have I. We'll go to the police.

Sherlock What? Those incompetent bunglers. Never!

John But Ruby's life's in danger. A mad scientist is manufacturing millions of monsters and a bunch of wholesale murderers is going around committing—wholesale murders.

Sherlock Yes, but never mind the trivial matters. It's these specialist antique thieves we must deal with first.

John Specialist antiq—? Mr Holmes, I'm beginning to think I made a serious mistake.

Sherlock I know, but never mind, leave everything to me.

John I mean, in employing you. You're nothing but a—a——oh, never mind. I'm off to the police.

He moves off R *with the wheelbarrow and the corpse*

Sherlock You'll spoil everything! This kind of case needs my particular deductive genius, my special—he's gone. I shall have to move quickly. But how to gain access to Enstein Hall? Simple. (*Wheeling himself quickly off* R) Another masterly disguise.

Black-out. The traverse tabs open

SCENE 5

Enstein Hall

The alcove curtains are closed. There is a chaise-longue LC, with a small table behind it. Mrs Burkenhare is discovered in silhouette. She holds a remote control unit and presses a button. Sweet music (tape effect), begins to play. She presses another button and soft lights come up on the chaise-longue. She presses a third button

A Footman Monster enters L with a tray on which is an ice bucket, containing a bottle of champagne, and two glasses, which he puts on the table and exits

Music 22: This Is My Way to Make a Man

Mrs Burkenhare   When other women have a headache,
Or complain of migraine,
I put on the soft lights
And get out the champagne.

I spray myself with perfume,
Let music fill the room.
I feel so disruptive,
So seductive.

And I will take him
And I will break him;
Whisper sweet nothings
In his ear;
Ply him with champagne,
Tell him it's all a game.
I am the mistress,
There's nothing to fear.

When he's perspiring
I'll call him "dahling"
And tell him to move me like no other man can.
I will stroke him
And provoke him
For this is my way to make a man.
Chase me——
A man!
For this is my way to make a man.

When other women say they're tired,
Or say they're overworked,
I drink to the future
And get on with my work.

I pucker my red lips
And then his hair I shall kiss.
I feel so attentive,
But never repentive.

You see,
I will take him ... *etc.*

When he's perspiring ... *etc.*
D'ye hear me?
A man!
D'ye hear me?
A man!
Don't lose me.
For this is my way to make a man,
A man!

She is lying back on the chaise-longue *looking very seductive as Frank bursts on* UC

Frank Leukie!
Mrs Burkenhare Frank!
Frank Baby, this is it!
Mrs Burkenhare At last!
Frank Yeah, at last—Gee, it's dark in here.

He produces his remote control unit and presses a button. The Lights come up

Mrs Burkenhare But, Frank——
Frank And kinda noisy.

He presses another button. The music (effect), stops

Mrs Burkenhare Frank, don't you understand?
Frank Sure, you've got a headache.
Mrs Burkenhare No. (*She sits up, glumly*) Not yet. I usually keep those for my husbands.
Frank You do? That's kinda thoughtful. But listen, Leukie, I've done it again. My biggest breakthrough yet. What man has been seeking for centuries. The secret of life itself, not just animation, but *re*animation. Bring me your dead and I'll make them live again!
Mrs Burkenhare But you do that already.
Frank Yeah, but only in bits and pieces. An arm from here, a leg from there and a head from somewhere else. Why, one monster might be made from a dozen different people. Now I can take them as they come! Fit a micro-chip control, put 'em in the machine and bingo! Life's rejects are reanimated!
Mrs Burkenhare You mean—no sorting, no stitching, no reassembly?
Frank That's right.
Mrs Burkenhare What a saving in time—what a saving in money! Every corpse a monster.
Frank Baby these won't just be monsters. They'll be second-hand people. Only better—they'll last forever.
Mrs Burkenhare Frank, we'll make a fortune. When can you start?
Frank Right now. I've re-programmed the machine and it's raring to go.

He presses a remote control button and the alcove curtains open to reveal the machine

Mrs Burkenhare Frank, you're a genius. How lucky I happen to have some champagne. Let's celebrate.

She sits him at one end of the chaise-longue

Frank Whatever you say, baby, but do something for me.
Mrs Burkenhare Certainly. What?
Frank Make mine a coke. I get all carried away with champagne.
Mrs Burkenhare You do? Then suddenly we're right out of coke. (*She fills a glass to the brim and hands it to him*) Cheers.

Frank Well, why not? Cheers. Here's looking at you.

They drink

Mrs Burkenhare And here's looking at you.
Frank At me? OK. Here's looking at me.

They drink

Mrs Burkenhare And here's to—to—reanimation.
Frank I'll drink to that. To reanimation.

They drink

Mrs Burkenhare (*refilling his glass*) And here's to—us.

She turns away to put the bottle down and restart the music effect with her remote control

Frank Yeah! Here's to—us.

They drink

You know what, Leukie? You're quite some broad.

She surreptitiously operates her remote control to lower the Lights and leans closer to him

Mrs Burkenhare And you're quite some man.

Igor and Mrs Body burst on R

Igor
Mrs Body } (*together*) Spies! Spies!

Mrs Burkenhare is leaning so close that she topples forward as Frank leaps up

Frank What's that?
Mrs Burkenhare Another failure.

She jabs at her remote control to make the Lights snap up and the music end in a sudden wail

Mrs Body Mr E!
Igor Mrs B!
Mrs Body Disaster!
Igor We're discovered!
Mrs Body Surrounded by spies!
Igor And they know everything!
Frank Hey now, take it easy. What do you mean, spies?
Mrs Body There were three of them.
Igor They got into the Dungeon of Death.
Mrs Burkenhare So? That's what it's there for, for people to get into.
Mrs Body Yes, but they got out again——
Igor Alive!
Mrs Body With the old master——
Igor Dead!

Frank The old master? How did he get there?
Igor In a wheelbarrow.
Frank A wheelbarrow?
Mrs Body Yes, and the spies took him as evidence.
Frank In the wheelbarrow?
Mrs Body No, they were in a wheelchair. Well, one of 'em was.
Igor With another one pushing it.
Frank The wheelchair?
Igor No, the wheelbarrow. It was that lawyer, young Mr Good.
Mrs Body Yes, he's Sherlock Holmes.
Frank Mr Good is?
Mrs Body No, he's his grandson.
Frank Whose grandson?
Mrs Body Sherlock Holmes's. Then there's a third one.
Mrs Burkenhare (*sarcastically*) Dr Watson, I presume.
Igor That's right. She's with Boris.
Mrs Burkenhare She? Dr Watson? With Boris? What is all this nonsense?
Mrs Body It's not nonsense. It's what your hubbies told us.
Mrs Burkenhare Then it is nonsense.

A front doorbell rings off R

Igor   } (*together*) It's them!
Mrs Body
Igor Run for your lives!
Mrs Body (*feeling her back*) Run?
Igor Walk quickly then.

They exit hurriedly L *as the doorbell sounds again*

Mrs Burkenhare (*moving* R) Everyone's gone mad. Wheelbarrows, wheelchairs, spies! Whoever heard of a spy in a wheelchair?

She exits R *and returns almost immediately*

My God!
Frank Who is it?
Mrs Burkenhare A spy in a wheelchair!

Sherlock propels himself on R, *preposterously disguised as an old-fashioned fireman with brass helmet, etc.*

Sherlock How do you do? I'm the fire inspector.
Frank You're what?
Sherlock The fire inspector. Don't you believe me? (*He rings a bell attached to his chair*)
Mrs Burkenhare Of course we do. (*Aside to Frank*) Humour him, he's mad. (*To Sherlock*) You're a lovely fire inspector.
Sherlock Thank you, madam. I knew I'd deceive you—that is, deceive you into thinking I didn't mean business, but I do. I've come to inspect your premises and particularly your stock of antique furniture.
Frank Antique furniture?

Sherlock Yes, very inflammable antique furniture. Especially when it's "hot".

Mrs Burkenhare But we haven't got any antique furniture.

Sherlock No? Then what about this *chaise-longue*? Obviously not a reproduction. Equally obviously there's been some restoration. Do a lot of that, don't you—restoring old things, bringing them back to life?

Mrs Burkenhare (*exchanging a look with Frank*) Maybe not so mad.

Sherlock In fact, I know you do. I've already inspected your other premises—that Dungeon place.

Mrs Burkenhare (*aside*) Leave him to me. I'm not called Leucretia for nothing. (*She looks at some large rings on her hands*) Hm, arsenic, I think. (*She opens a ring to poison one of the glasses*)

Sherlock So now I know everything, your whole dastardly plot, because I am none other than—(*he tries to remove his helmet*)—than——Could you just ease the chin strap off for me?

Frank does so

Thank you. Yes, none other than—Sherlock Holmes Junior!

Mrs Burkenhare Congratulations. Have some champagne. (*She hands him the poisoned glass*)

Sherlock How kind. Obviously you realize it's useless to try to deceive a master detective like myself. (*Raising the glass*) Your health.

Mrs Burkenhare (*reciprocating*) Yours.

John tears in R with the wheelbarrow and corpse

John Stop!

Frank A wheelbarrow!

Mrs Burkenhare (*opening a second ring*) Strychnine. (*She starts lacing the drink she is holding*)

Frank Great-uncle!

John Nobody move! I've got the place surrounded.

Sherlock Too late, my boy. I've already solved the case.

John Twaddle!

Mrs Burkenhare I know, but we must humour him. Have some champagne.

John Thank you. No, no!

Sherlock I'll have it then. (*He takes the other glass*)

John (*snatching both glasses and putting them on the small table*) This is no time for shilly-shallying with champagne.

Mrs Burkenhare Pity.

Frank What are you doing with Great-uncle?

John Stuff your great-uncle! Where's Ruby?

Mrs Burkenhare Who's Ruby?

Sherlock He means Watson.

John I mean Ruby. But I'm not wasting any time. (*He blows a whistle*)

A number of Police rush onstage

Arrest them!

Frank I want to see my lawyer!

John I am your lawyer.
Frank Oh, shucks!

An Inspector, with two more Constables who have Igor and Mrs Body in custody, enter L

Igor
Mrs Body } *(together)* Let go!
Put me down!

Igor
Mrs Body } *(together)* Ooh, the old master!

Inspector *(to John)* That's the lot, sir. We'll get them all down to the station.
Frank Wait! For everybody's safety let me switch off this machinery. It could be dangerous.
John Oh, very well.

Frank presses some buttons on his remote control. Immediately the Police drop those they are holding and grab John and Sherlock instead

Hey, what's going on? You're arresting us.
Sherlock I told you the police were incompetent bunglers.
Frank No, I just happened to recognize them. They're a batch we sold to Scotland Yard. *(He presses a button)* An armed batch.

The Police produce pistols which they level at John and Sherlock

So now——

Before he can press another button there is a loud scream off R *and Boris enters dragging Ruby*

Boris Hullo. Here, where do her electrodes fit?
Ruby Not where you thought, anyway! *(She rubs her ear painfully)* Ooh!
John Ruby!
Ruby John!
Frank Well done, Boris. Now we've got all of them.
Mrs Burkenhare Yes, we can kill them altogether.
Boris Kill? You can't do that, silly. She's a monster.
John How dare you talk like that about the woman I love!
Ruby Oh, John, do you really?
John Yes, really. And when we get out of this I want you to be——
Frank Shut up, both of you. Sorry, Boris, but she's not a monster.
Boris Well, she ought to be. I want one just like her.
Frank OK, Boris, no problem. As soon as I've killed her I'll reanimate her for you.
Boris When?
Frank Oh, in just a while, but——
Boris Now.
Frank I can't, Boris, because——
Boris NOW!
Frank But it's on command mode and——
Boris I'll do it then.

He grabs the remote control unit and jabs at it. The Police swing round to threaten Frank and Mrs Burkenhare

Frank ⎫
Mrs Burkenhare ⎰ (*together*) Boris!

Boris makes another jab, the Police swing back and Frank and Mrs Burkenhare give a sigh of relief

Frank Whew! Now just give me——

Boris starts jabbing furiously, the Police swing rapidly to and fro to assorted cries from the two groups. As this is happening—

Igor The old master! Now's our chance!

He and Mrs Body start to wheel the corpse away

Mrs Body Where shall we—?

They see they are being threatened by the Police and freeze until the Police move again

Igor In here, quick!

They disappear with the corpse into the machine. Boris stops jabbing and the Police finally come to rest aiming at Frank and Mrs Burkenhare

Boris Rotten thing. Only one more button to try.
Frank Boris, not that one! Don't touch that——

Boris does. The Police shoot, hitting Frank and Mrs Burkenhare

Boris Noisy that one. Still doesn't work though.

   He throws down the unit and stomps off L

   The Police become confused and run off L *and* R

Mrs Burkenhare falls back on the chaise-longue

Mrs Burkenhare Frank! Frank! I'm dying!
Frank So what? So am I. (*He falls on top of her*)
Mrs Burkenhare Oh, Frank, at last, but too late, too—— (*She gives an expiring gasp and dies*)
John Golly! They did it! They shot them!
Sherlock With those idiot police it's lucky it wasn't us.
Ruby Never mind, it's all over, we're safe now.

   Burke enters R, *levelling a drawn pistol*

Burke That's what you think. Hands up!

They comply

   Willie! Look what I've found.

   Hare enters R

Hare (*as he enters*) The Firing Squad?
Burke No, them spies. Won't that please the missis and Mr E?
Sherlock I doubt it. (*He points to the* chaise-longue) They're dead.

Burke }
Hare } *(together)* What!?

They rush to the chaise-longue. *Burke bends over trying to hear a heartbeat. John and Ruby realize they have a chance to escape and edge away, taking Sherlock with them*

Hare Glory be and save us all! They can't be dead, not really dead. Willie, tell me they're not dead.
Burke They're dead.
Hare Waaaah! It's too much! My little wife! Dead! And it's Thursday, my turn for her to have a headache! I can't stand it! I'll never get over it!
Burke Calm down, Willie. Here, have a drink. We'll both have a drink.

They pick up the two glasses of champagne

Hare Willie, how did they die?
Burke That's the worst part about it. They were killed.
Hare Killed! Who by? Just tell me who by!
Sherlock *(almost at the exit)* Well, I don't like to boast, but——
John }
Ruby } *(together)* Shut up!
Burke }   *(together)*
Hare } *(together)* The spies!
Burke Of course! Stay where you are and come back here!
Hare What shall we do with them, Willie?
Burke What they always do with spies. Shoot them at dawn.
Hare It's a lovely thought, but I don't think I can wait that long. Let's shoot them now.
Burke I'll drink to that. Cheers.
Hare Bottoms up.

They drink

Burke }
Hare } *(together)* Right——

Burke clutches his stomach and Hare his throat

Willie——aaahhh!

They die

Ruby The drinks—poisoned!
Sherlock Of course. My acute sense of smell told me they were.
John What? But you wanted to——
Ruby Never mind, John. Somehow we were saved.
Sherlock Naturally. After all, we were in the right so nothing could hurt us.
Officer Monster *(off* R*)* Fire!

Shots. All, to their astonishment, have been hit

The Firing Squad run across from R *to* L *and exit*

Sherlock Watson, perhaps I was wrong after all.
Ruby Elementary, my dear Holmes.

Sherlock slumps in his chair, John and Ruby slump to the floor

After a slight pause, Boris enters L

Boris (*looking around*) They've all run out of juice. Funny, I didn't think people did. And I still haven't got anybody to plug in with. I wonder if this does anything.

He pulls a large lever on the machine. Lights flash and electronic noises

The Police and Firing Squad rush in and start milling around

There are shouts from Igor and Mrs Body, who emerge hurriedly from the machine

Igor
Mrs Body } Boris!

Igor (*frantically working levers on the machine*) You shouldn't have done that, Boris!

Suddenly everything stops

Thank goodness! 'Cos in there, there's——

The machine emits a new noise, which builds to a crescendo and a sign "REANIMATE" starts flashing

When the crescendo is reached there is a brief pause and the Corpse walks out of the machine

Boris Daddy!
Igor The old master!
Mrs Body Alive again!
Corpse Exactly.
Igor And walking——
Corpse Of course.
Mrs Body Talking——
Corpse Naturally.
Boris Just like us.
Corpse No, Boris. (*He indicates the audience*) Just like them. (*To the audience*) Well, I told you it could happen. (*He picks up Mrs Burkenhare's remote control*) And with my great-nephew's little improvements—(*he presses some buttons*)—it has! (*He presses a final button*)

Music 23: Finale Medley

The Police and the Firing Squad spring into life and load all the dead principals into the machine

All   Eat, drink, breathe, think,
                   Run, hop, lean, blink,

The Humanoid Boogie's
Coming home to roost.
Jump, stride, squirm, walk,
Shout, scream, nod, talk,
It's really something else,
It's gonna be a hoot.

Going,
We want to dance and sing,
Dancing,
We're not an awful thing.

The dead principals start re-emerging from the machine, but moving in Monster fashion

Dead   We've come alive and we're feeling new,
Principals We're walking, talking, just like you, just like you.
Tutti   Walking, talking, walking, talking,
                Just like you, just like you.
                Walking, talking, walking, talking,
                Just like you, just like you.

                Humanoid, humanoid boogie,
                Humanoid, humanoid boogie,
                Humanoid, humanoid boogie
                Humanoid.

                Total! Built-in control!
                Total built-in control.

                Personally speaking,
                There is no rust or squeaking,
                No need for any maintenance
                Or old oil can.

                Total independence, we're in attendance,
                To do most anything a human can!
                Do most anything a human can!
                Do most anything a human can!

Drum break

Gaily, daily, dealing out death,
Wotta lot we got,
We're all short of breath.
Insanely, humanely, we'll do our best,
It's over in a trice,
They are put to rest.

They can grope at the rope,
They can mope down the slope,

But when all is done and said
Everyone will end up dead;
It's the end,
There's no hope!
It's the end,
There's no hope!

It's a pleasure,
You're a treasure,
We give new meaning
To government cuts.
At our leisure
We will measure
You for the chopping block
With no ifs or buts.

Instrumental

It's the end, there's no hope!
It's the end, there's no hope!
It's the end, there's no hope!
It's the end, there's no hope!

It's the end, there's no hope!
It's the end, there's no hope!

There must be a way
There must be a way
There must be a way,
There must be a way.

There must be a way,
There must be a way *etc.*

There must be a way for me to get hold of you,
My little monster!
There must be a way to find another kind of me.
There must be!

You're so fiendish, you're so horrible
You're so grotesque, it is wonderful.
There must be a way for me to get hold of you
For me to get hold of you
For me to get hold of you

If there's a way we'll find it
If it cuts up rough we'll grind it
Throw ourselves into the fray
Get on our knees and pray.

If there's a way we're gonna find it
We're gonna find it.

We are the way
The future is ours you'll see
We are the way,
The future is ours you'll see

There must be a way,
There must be a way,
There must be a way,
There must be a way *etc.*

CURTAIN

FURNITURE AND PROPERTY LIST

ACT I

SCENE 1

On stage: Table. *On it:* trick coffin containing prop corpse and old book
Chair
Alcove curtains closed. *Behind them:* table with electrodes attached, ancient-looking electrical equipment

Off stage: Candlestick with lighted candle **(Igor)**
Briefcase with legal papers **(John)**

When traverse tabs close on page 16:

Strike: Table
Candlestick

Table and electrical equipment from alcove

Re-set: Chair

Set: Desk. *On it*: Yellow Pages directory
Notice hanging down—"GOOD, BETTER & BEST, SOLICITORS"
Close alcove curtains

Off stage: Prop corpse **(Mrs Body** and **Igor)**

SCENE 2

Strike: Notice

Set: Chair ⎫ could be re-set from SCENE 1
Desk ⎭
Portrait of solid Victorian-looking gentleman

Off stage: File of papers **(Ruby)**
Wheelchair, Calabash pipe **(Sherlock)**

SCENE 3

Strike: Portrait

Set: Notice hanging down in front of traverse tabs—"ENSTEIN FUNERAL PARLOUR"
Desk ⎫ could be re-set from SCENE 2
Chair ⎭

On desk: telephone, message pad, pencil
Potted palm

Plinth
Alcove curtains closed. *Behind them:* large machine with lights and dials
   labelled ASSEMBLY, STITCHING, ANIMATION, CONTROL and
   switches marked HEAD, TORSO, ARMS, LEGS

Off stage: Coffin **(Burke** and **Hare)**
Prop corpse **(Igor** and **Mrs Body)**
2 legs **(Stage Management)**
Leg **(Igor)**

When traverse tabs close on page 28:

Strike: Notice
Desk
Chair
Plinth
Potted palm
Legs
Coffin
Set: Alcove curtains closed

ACT II

SCENE 1

On stage: Notice hanging down—"ENSTEIN ENTERPRISES"
Desks with typewriters ⎤
Tables with telephones ⎦ could be painted cut-outs
Telephone

Off stage: Bundles of orders **(Male Monsters)**
Remote control unit **(Frank)**

SCENE 2

Strike: Desks and typewriters
Tables and telephones
Bundles of orders
Notice

Off stage: Tray of matches with sign "MATCHES", dark glasses, wheelchair
   (Sherlock)

SCENE 3

Set: Notice hanging down—"DUNGEON OF DEATH. PANORAMA OF
   EXECUTION THROUGH THE AGES"
Electric chair
Execution block and prop axe
Guillotine
Low screen with chute set into it
Basket at foot of chute
Bell push labelled "FIRING SQUAD"
Sign on door "WAY OUT"

Off stage: Noose **(Boris)**
Arrow **(Stage Management)**—required 3 times
Wheelbarrow and prop corpse **(Mrs Body)**
Wheelchair **(Sherlock)**
Axe **(Hare)**
Prop heads **(Stage Management)**

Personal: **Officer Monster:** sword
Firing Squad Monsters: rifles
Burke: pistol
Hare: pistol

SCENE 4

Strike: Notice
Signs
Electric chair
Guillotine
Low screen and chute
Basket with heads

Set: Notice hanging down—"A STREET"

Off stage: Wheelchair **(Sherlock)**
Wheelbarrow and corpse **(John)**
Wheelchair, wheelbarrow and corpse **(Sherlock)**
Notice—"FURTHER ALONG THE STREET" **(Stage Management)**
Wheelbarrow and corpse **(John)**
Notice—"ROUND THE CORNER" **(Stage Management)**
Wheelchair **(Sherlock)**

Personal: **Officer Monster:** sword
Firing Squad Monsters: rifles

SCENE 5

Strike: Notice

Set: *Chaise-longue*
Small table. *On it:* remote control unit **(for Mrs Burkenhare)**
Alcove curtains closed. *Behind them:* machine with lights, dials, levers

Off stage: Tray with 2 glasses, ice-bucket containing bottle of champagne **(Footman Monster)**
Remote control unit **(Frank)**
Wheelchair with bell fitted **(Sherlock)**
Wheelbarrow and corpse, whistle **(John)**

Personal: **Mrs Burkenhare:** 2 poison rings
Police: pistols
Burke: pistol
Hare: pistol
Officer Monster: sword
Firing Squad Monsters: rifles

LIGHTING PLOT

Practical fittings required: Machine with lights
Various simple interior and exterior settings

ACT I

To open: Black-out

Cue 1	After **Music 2: Spooky Incidental** begins *Spot on coffin* C	(Page 1)
Cue 2	**Corpse:** ". . . perfect in every detail——" *Spot on Monster* R	(Page 1)
Cue 3	**Corpse:** ". . . they'll make two——" *Spot on two Monsters* L	(Page 1)
Cue 4	**Corpse:** "Or three——" *Spot on 3rd Monster* L	(Page 1)
Cue 5	**Corpse:** "Or more!" *Spot on 4th Monster* L	(Page 1)
Cue 6	**Corpse:** "Lots more!" *Lights up on remaining Monsters*	(Page 1)
Cue 7	At end of **Music 4: Humanoid Boogie** *Fade to spot on coffin* C	(Page 3)
Cue 8	When **Corpse** lowers coffin lid *Fade to Black-out*	(Page 3)
Cue 9	When traverse tabs are open *Lightning flash*	(Page 3)
Cue 10	As **Igor** enters *Bring up general lighting. Lightning flash*	(Page 3)
Cue 11	**Igor:** ". . . so I do. Lovely." *Lightning flash*	(Page 3)
Cue 12	**Frank:** ". . . the name. Frank Enstein." *Lightning flash*	(Page 4)
Cue 13	**Frank:** "Enstein. Frank Enstein." *Lightning flash*	(Page 5)
Cue 14	**Frank:** ". . . way to spend a night." *Lightning flash*	(Page 7)
Cue 15	**Mrs Body:** "If it does——!" *Lightning flash*	(Page 8)

Cue 16	**Frank:** "Then how in Hades——?" *Lightning flash*	(Page 9)
Cue 17	**Mrs Body:** "... the storm's passing over." *Very big lightning flash*	(Page 9)
Cue 18	As **Frank** pushes third lever *Lights flicker*	(Page 9)
Cue 19	**All** exit at end of reprise of **Music 9: Every Home Should Have** ... *etc.* *Fade to light on* **John**	(Page 17)
Cue 20	**John:** "No. Think, think!" *Fade light on* **John**	(Page 17)
Cue 21	After muffled thumpings and bangings off L *Bring up lights downstage*	(Page 17)
Cue 22	When **Frank** and **Boris** exit R *Crossfade to light on* **John**	(Page 17)
Cue 23	**John:** "... Sherlock Holmes—Junior?" *Black-out*	(Page 18)
Cue 24	At start of SCENE 2 *Bring up full lighting*	(Page 18)
Cue 25	**John:** "... when I went to Enstein Hall." *Fade to Black-out, hold for agreed time then bring lights up to full again*	(Page 20)
Cue 26	**Ruby:** "... in a funeral parlour." *Black-out*	(Page 20)
Cue 27	At start of SCENE 3 *Spot on sign "ENSTEIN FUNERAL PARLOUR" then bring up downstage lighting*	(Page 21)
Cue 28	At end of **Music 12: I'm Only Monstrous** as tabs open *Bring up all lighting to full*	(Page 22)
Cue 29	As alcove curtains open *Start lights winking on machine*	(Page 23)
Cue 30	**Frank:** "Head!" *Snap on machine light 1*	(Page 23)
Cue 31	**Frank:** "Torso!" *Snap on machine light 2*	(Page 23)
Cue 32	**Frank:** "Arms!" *Snap on machine light 3*	(Page 23)
Cue 33	**Frank:** "Legs!" *Snap on machine light 4*	(Page 23)
Cue 34	**Frank:** "Assembly!" *Snap on machine light 5*	(Page 23)
Cue 35	**Frank:** "Stitching!" *Snap on machine light 6*	(Page 23)

Cue 36	**Frank:** "Animation!"	(Page 23)
	Snap on machine light 7	
Cue 37	**Boris:** "... got something missing. But somehow——"	(Page 28)
	Fade to spot on **Boris**	
Cue 38	**Boris** (*singing*): "Me to get hold of you."	(Page 29)
	Spots on **Monsters** *as they enter* DS	
Cue 39	**Boris** (*singing*): "To find another kind of me."	(Page 29)
	Spot on Burke and Hare	
Cue 40	**Burke** and **Hare** (*singing*): "Nice 'n' sleazy."	(Page 29)
	Spot on Sherlock	
Cue 41	**Sherlock** (*singing*): "Respected."	(Page 29)
	Spot on Mrs Burkenhare	
Cue 42	**Mrs Burkenhare** (*singing*): "Affected."	(Page 29)
	Spot on **Igor** *and* **Mrs Body**	
Cue 43	**Igor** and **Mrs Body** (*singing*): "Where to save him."	(Page 29)
	Spot on Frank	
Cue 44	**Frank** (*singing*): "My monsters."	(Page 30)
	Spot on **Ruby** *and* **John**	

ACT II

To open: Full general lighting

Cue 45	**Ruby:** "... 'The Dungeon of Death'!"	(Page 36)
	Black-out	
Cue 46	At start of SCENE 3	(Page 36)
	Bring up dim lighting and noose and gallows shadow effect; then on agreed timing snap up to full	
Cue 47	As **Boris** staggers into electric chair	(Page 38)
	Start flashing tube lights; cut when **Hare** *switches it off*	
Cue 48	During **Music 19: Put Your Head Upon the Block** whenever a **Tourist** sits in the electric chair	(Page 44)
	Flashing tube lights	
Cue 49	As **Burke** and **Hare** run off R	(Page 45)
	Black-out	
Cue 50	At start of SCENE 4	(Page 46)
	Bring up lighting downstage	
Cue 51	**Burke:** "... every one of them. Come on!"	(Page 46)
	Start strobe lantern	
Cue 52	At end of chase	(Page 46)
	Stop strobe lantern	
Cue 53	**Sherlock:** "Another masterly disguise."	(Page 49)
	Black-out	

Cue 54   At start of SCENE 5   (Page 49)
            Bring up lights to silhouette Mrs Burkenhare

Cue 55   When **Mrs Burkenhare** operates her remote control the second   (Page 49)
                time
            Bring up soft lighting on chaise-longue

Cue 56   When **Frank** operates his remote control unit   (Page 51)
            Snap lights up to full

Cue 57   **Frank:** "You're quite some broad."   (Page 52)
            Fade to soft lighting on chaise-longue

Cue 58   As **Mrs Burkenhare** jabs at her remote control unit   (Page 52)
            Snap lights up to full

Cue 59   As **Boris** pulls large lever   (Page 58)
            Start lights on machine flashing

Cue 60   **Igor:** "'Cos in there, there's——"   (Page 58)
            Start "Reanimate" sign on machine flashing

EFFECTS PLOT

ACT I

Cue 1   After CURTAIN has risen   (Page 1)
         Howling wind and storm effects—fade gradually

Cue 2   Traverse tabs open; lightning   (Page 3)
         Thunder

Cue 3   **Igor** enters; lightning   (Page 3)
         Thunder

Cue 4   **Igor:** ". . . so I do. Lovely." Lightning   (Page 3)
         Thunder

Cue 5   **Frank:** ". . . the name. Frank Enstein." Lightning   (Page 4)
         Thunder

Cue 6   **Frank:** "Enstein. Frank Enstein." Lightning   (Page 5)
         Thunder

Cue 7   **John:** "Not a crumb."   (Page 7)
         Deep-toned bell chimes the hour then strikes 12

Cue 8   As **Igor** opens coffin lid   (Page 7)
         Creak

Cue 9   **Frank:** ". . . to spend a night." Lightning   (Page 7)
         Thunder and muted rumblings continuing under **Music 6: Spooky
         Incidental**

Cue 10   **Mrs Body:** "If it does——!" Lightning   (Page 8)
         Thunder

Cue 11   **Frank:** "Then how in Hades——?" Lightning   (Page 8)
         Thunder

Cue 12   **Mrs Body:** ". . . the storm's passing over." Lightning   (Page 9)
         Thunder, very loud

Cue 13   As **Frank** pushes third lever   (Page 9)
         Electronic noises, fizzles and smoke, building to an explosion

Cue 14   **Frank:** "Who's Mrs Burkenhare?"   (Page 15)
         *Sound of car approaching very fast followed by a scream of
         brakes and the slam of a car door*

Cue 15   As traverse tabs close   (Page 17)
         Muffled thumpings and bangings off L

Cue 16   At start of SCENE 2   (Page 18)
         Sound of violin badly played

Cue 17	**Ruby:** "Are you there, Mr Holmes?" *Stop violin*	(Page 18)
Cue 18	Lights fade to Black-out *Bring up sound of clock ticking; hold at agreed level for agreed time then fade as Lights come up*	(Page 20)
Cue 19	**John:** "What can I do?" *Stop ticking*	(Page 20)
Cue 20	**Burke:** ". . . my little darling." *Telephone rings*	(Page 22)
Cue 21	As alcove curtains open *Burble of electronic noises*	(Page 23)

Cue 22	**Frank:** "Head!"	
Cue 23	**Frank:** "Torso!"	*Each command is*
Cue 24	**Frank:** "Arms!"	*accompanied by*
Cue 25	**Frank:** "Legs!"	*a different electronic*
Cue 26	**Frank:** "Assembly!"	*noise*
Cue 27	**Frank:** "Stitching!"	

(Page 23)

| Cue 28 | **Frank:** "Animation!"
 Several wild noises ending in a belch | (Page 23) |
| Cue 29 | **Mrs Burkenhare:** ". . . the right premises, and then——"
 Loud crashing and banging like a pile of falling logs | (Page 27) |

ACT II

Cue 30	As Curtain rises *Rhythmic typing and telephones ringing*	(Page 31)
Cue 31	**Mrs Body:** ". . . keeps 'em rolling in." *Telephone rings*	(Page 32)
Cue 32	**Boris:** ". . . one, two, three, jump!" *Loud crash off R*	(Page 38)
Cue 33	As **Hare** switches on electric chair *Crackling noises; cut as **Hare** switches it off*	(Page 38)
Cue 34	When guillotine blade disappears behind screen *Sickening thud*	(Page 39)
Cue 35	**Officer Monster:** "Fire!" *Salvo of shots, with ricochets*	(Page 39)
Cue 36	**Igor** opens "WAY OUT" door *Dry ice effect from within*	(Page 40)
Cue 37	As **Sherlock** enters *Wheelchair squeak*	(Page 40)
Cue 38	As **Burke** staggers into electric chair *Crackling noises; cut when **Hare** switches it off*	(Page 42)

Cue 39   When guillotine blade descends behind screen   (Page 44)
          Thud

Cue 40   **Officer Monster:** "Fire!"   (Page 44)
          Salvo of shots

Cue 41   During **Music 19: Put Your Head Upon the Block**   (Page 44)
          Crackling noises whenever a **Tourist** *sits in the electric chair; thud
          whenever guillotine blade descends*

Cue 42   **Officer Monster:** "Fire!"   (Page 45)
          Salvo of shots

Cue 43   When **Mrs Burkenhare** operates her remote control unit   (Page 49)
          Sweet music

Cue 44   When **Frank** operates his remote control unit (2nd time) (Page 51)
          Stop music

Cue 45   When **Mrs Burkenhare** operates her remote control unit   (Page 52)
          Sweet music

Cue 46   When **Mrs Burkenhare** jabs at her remote control unit   (Page 52)
          Stop music with sudden wail

Cue 47   **Mrs Burkenhare:** "Then it is nonsense."   (Page 53)
          Door bell off R

Cue 48   **Igor:** "Walk quickly, then."   (Page 53)
          Doorbell off R

Cue 49   **Frank:** "Don't touch that—"   (Page 56)
          Pistol shots

Cue 50   **Officer Monster** (*off*): "Fire!"   (Page 57)
          Salvo of shots

Cue 51   As **Boris** pulls large lever   (Page 58)
          Electronic noises from machine

Cue 52   **Igor:** "... shouldn't have done that, Boris!"   (Page 58)
          Noises stop suddenly

Cue 53   **Igor:** "'Cos in there, there's——"   (Page 58)
          New electronic noise building to a crescendo

MADE AND PRINTED IN GREAT BRITAIN BY
LATIMER TREND & COMPANY LTD PLYMOUTH
MADE IN ENGLAND